T0079790

A LIBRARY
MISCELLANY

A
LIBRARY
MISCELLANY

Claire Cock-Starkey

Bodleian Library
UNIVERSITY OF OXFORD

First published in 2018 by the Bodleian Library
Broad Street, Oxford OX1 3BG

www.bodleianshop.co.uk

ISBN   978 1 85124 472 0

Text © Claire Cock-Starkey, 2018

Claire Cock-Starkey has asserted her right to be identified as the author
of this Work.

All rights reserved

The poem on page 73 is reproduced here with the kind permission of
Cheltenham Ladies' College Archive

No part of this book may be reproduced, stored in a retrieval system,
or transmitted in any form or by any means, electronic, mechanical,
photocopying, recording, or otherwise, without the written permission
of the Bodleian Library, except for the purpose of research or private
study, or criticism or review.

Cover design by Dot Little at the Bodleian Library
Designed and typeset in 11 on 13 Perpetua by illuminati, Grosmont
Printed and bound in China by C&C Offset Printing Co. Ltd
on 100 gsm Yulong pure 1.3 paper

British Library Catalogue in Publishing Data
A CIP record of this publication is available from the British Library

INTRODUCTION

Italian writer Umberto Eco once said that the most valuable books in the library are those we have yet to read. Eco is here reminding us that our knowledge is as infinite as the books that exist – to encounter a library full of books we have not read is to be offered an unparalleled resource of knowledge and possibilities.

Libraries by their very existence invite us to explore, enjoy and engage with books. The very first libraries were open only to scholars, but today learning has been democratized and public libraries open to everyone are held dear the world over.

Many of these wonderful spaces allow children their first experience of books and reading, and can have a profound influence over a child's future relationship with books. The excitement and joy of a childhood trip to the library is a collective memory many can relate to.

Libraries are not just repositories for books. Many libraries also hold objects such as coins, medals and curios; maps; music; ephemera; patents and photographs. And some libraries hold very few books indeed, choosing to specialize in other areas, such as art libraries, herbaria or the library of smells, the Osmothèque.

Libraries come in all shapes and sizes, from the most ancient and august university library to the tiniest village library housed in an old phone box. Circulating libraries, mobile libraries, public libraries, academic libraries and even paperless libraries – *A Library Miscellany* honours them all.

History has shown that as long as there have been books and writing, there have been people who have collected those books and created libraries. The urge to collect and share our cultural history is, it seems, irresistible. Many libraries owe their existence to an individual, such as Andrew Carnegie, Sir Thomas Bodley, J.P. Morgan, Henry E. Huntington – people with a vision who shared their passion for books with the world. Their legacies are highlighted in *A Library Miscellany*, and so too are the stories behind the personal libraries of some extraordinary individuals, such as John Dee and Charles Darwin.

A library collection is not just about the books and manuscripts held within its walls; it also reflects how that collection has been ordered, organized, classified and displayed. The art of librarianship is explored in *A Library Miscellany*, with entries explaining the vagaries of the Dewey Decimal Classification System, the mysteries of the shelfmark and the story behind legal deposit. Good librarians are crucial to the usability of any library; the right systems allow readers to navigate and explore dauntingly large collections, to identify the right book on the right subject, and – thanks to systems such as 'serendipitous browsing', whereby books on similar subjects are shelved together – finding one useful book on the shelf will hopefully lead on to another, and another.

A Library Miscellany does not just look at libraries as a whole but also singles out some of the greatest library treasures from collections around the world. The Book of Kells; the real Winnie-the-Pooh; the first dated printed book, the Diamond Sutra; the first book to be printed in North America, the Bay Psalm Book; and the first book with moveable type to be printed in Europe, the Gutenberg Bible – all are included.

The quirkier aspects of our libraries have not been ignored. Entries on the most borrowed library books, the largest library fine, the RMS *Titanic* library, fictional libraries of note, lost libraries, book thefts, New York Public Library's lions and the Vatican's secret archive await the avid fact-fan.

There is great comfort in the existence of libraries – just knowing that our cultural knowledge, history and literary output are protected, organized and available to anyone gives solace. This book celebrates all libraries great and small, so please dip in and enjoy this extended love letter to the library.

THE TEN LARGEST LIBRARIES
IN THE WORLD

Because libraries catalogue materials differently, it is not always easy to determine the size of library solely by the number of items it contains. For example, one library might catalogue a group of 100 related papers under one entry, whereas another will catalogue each item separately. There is thus enormous variation in the purported size of libraries purely as a result of cataloguing practice. However, based on libraries' own published statistics, the largest libraries in 2017 were:

LIBRARY	LOCATION	ITEMS
1. Library of Congress	Washington DC	162 m
2. The British Library	London	150 m
3. Library and Archives Canada	Ottawa	54 m
4. New York Public Library	New York	53 m
5. Russian State Library	Moscow	44 m
6. Bibliothèque nationale de France	Paris	40 m
7. National Library of Russia	St Petersburg	37 m
8. National Diet Library	Kyoto/Tokyo, Japan	36 m
9. Royal Danish Library	Copenhagen	35 m
10. National Library of China	Beijing	34 m

THE UN LIBRARY'S
MOST POPULAR BOOK

In December 2015 the United Nations Library in New York, the Dag Hammarskjöld Library, revealed that its most popular new book in 2015 was *Immunity for Heads of State and State Officials for International Crimes* by Dr Ramona Pedretti. Eyebrows were immediately raised as to why UN staff and delegates were borrowing a book which discusses the immunity of heads of state from international law. Representatives of the library quickly clarified that although Dr Pedretti's thesis had been the most popular new book, being borrowed twice and browsed four times, the most popular book in the collection had been the rather more inspiring *I Am Malala* by Malala Yousafzai.

LOST LIBRARIES

Unfortunately, due to war, natural disasters or fire, some very special libraries have been lost. Below are five libraries that have been destroyed:

LIBRARIES OF TIMBUKTU   The ancient libraries in Timbuktu, Mali, a centre of Islamic thought and learning from the thirteenth to the seventeenth century, were home to many important and ancient manuscripts on Islamic laws, history and ideas. Many times over the years the libraries, some housed in the homes of prominent local families, have come under threat of attack and so the precious manuscripts have been repeatedly packed into cases and buried in the sand. Sadly in 2013, a group of militants attacked and set fire to two of the libraries in Timbuktu. It was feared that the treasures may have been lost, but fortunately the locals had managed to pack away 400,000 of the valuable documents in metal cases, which were then locked with two keys and systematically dispersed over many months, hidden among traders' goods for safekeeping, in the capital Bamako. It is hoped that over time the collections may be safely brought back together.

GLASGOW SCHOOL OF ART LIBRARY   The iconic art nouveau library designed by Charles Rennie Mackintosh was destroyed by a fire in 2014. Much of the exterior of the building, which first opened in 1909, survived the flames but a large part of the beautiful interior, replete with stylized wood panelling and carved wooden desks, was lost. Fortunately much of the contents of the library and many students' works were saved by the quick action of the firefighters. A fierce debate followed on the future of the building, with some calling for full restoration, others entreating that Mackintosh himself would have wanted to see the space move forwards and a new library designed. In April 2015 it was announced the library would be faithfully restored to its former glory.

ANCIENT LIBRARY AT ALEXANDRIA   Established at the start of the third century BCE, the ancient library at Alexandria, Egypt, was said to be a centre of classical learning and is thought to have contained some 700,000 scrolls. That the library was destroyed is clear, but when exactly has been lost in the mists of time. Because a number of accounts of the destruction of the library survive from different time periods it seems likely that it was broken up over a number of years. Plutarch was the first to mourn its end, writing in 48 BCE that it had been accidentally burned down by Julius Caesar's troops during a siege, but others suggest it was Emperor Theodosius I in 391 CE who, in his quest to end paganism, had the building ruined. Some accounts suggest it was destroyed even later by invading Muslims in 640 CE. It is interesting to note that, despite the documentary evidence for the library, archaeologists have thus far found scant physical evidence for the library complex, leading some historians to posit that the library may never have existed at all.

THE NATIONAL LIBRARY OF BAGHDAD   In 2003 during the invasion of Iraq the National Library of Baghdad was engulfed in flames, resulting in the loss of countless priceless manuscripts, books and newspapers. It is estimated that 60 per cent of the library's archive and 25 per cent of the books were lost in the resulting chaos. The library has since been rebuilt and has recently been digitizing its remaining stock in an effort to preserve it for centuries to come.

LIBRARY OF CONGRESS   The world-famous Library of Congress in Washington DC was ravaged by fire on Christmas Eve, 1851. Some two-thirds of the library's 55,000 volumes were lost in the fire, including the majority of Thomas Jefferson's personal library, which the library had acquired in 1815. Fortunately Congress was quick to respond to the loss and raised funds to replace many of the lost books. Today the Library of Congress is one of the world's largest libraries, with over 17 million books in its collection.

PUBLIC LIBRARIES' LENDING CHANGES

The following statistics from the Chartered Institute of Public Finance and Accountancy (CIPFA) reveal how borrowing at public libraries in the UK has changed over a decade (2003/04–2013/14).

BORROWING	2003/04	2013/14
Children's books	86,792,620	89,169,968
Adult fiction	168,433,713	106,987,071
Adult non-fiction	85,700,275	51,087,684
All book issues	340,926,608	247,244,723

To put this in perspective, in 2003/04 there were 4,622 public libraries with a self-generated income (excluding authority funding) of £111,225,000 but by 2013/14 this had dropped to 4,145 public libraries with an income of £85,136,000.

SOME FICTIONAL LIBRARIES OF NOTE

Many literary works, films and television shows have featured libraries which stretch the realms of the imagination, creating fictional spaces that have become well loved by the public.

THE LIBRARY OF BABEL   *The Library of Babel* (or *La Biblioteca de Babel*) is a 1941 short story by Argentinian writer Jorge Luis Borges (1899–1986). Borges imagines a universe housing an infinite library full of every book ever written and yet equally full of complete gibberish. The librarians are thus endlessly searching for meaningful books.

HOGWARTS LIBRARY   The scene of many plot-hatching sessions in the *Harry Potter* series of books by J.K. Rowling. Full of magical texts on potions, wandlore and history, Hogwarts Library is central to Harry, Hermione and Ron's battle against Voldemort.

SUNNYDALE HIGH LIBRARY   The library which features in the highly popular 1990s' television show *Buffy the Vampire Slayer* is unfortunately sited above the entrance to the ominous Hellmouth. Fortunately the affable librarian is on hand to furnish Buffy with numerous texts on vanquishing demons and whatnot.

UNSEEN UNIVERSITY LIBRARY   The Unseen University Library was created by Terry Pratchett for his

Discworld series. The library is filled with limitless shelves full of books on magic, history, philosophy and books that have yet to be written. In Discworld books are a huge source of magical power, warping space and time, and so the library itself is a hub of magic. The librarian is an orang-utan and therefore is rather handy at getting books from high shelves.

THE SECRETUM   The monastic library created by Umberto Eco for *The Name of the Rose* (1980) is the largest library in the Christian world but accessible only to the librarian and his assistant. The library is based upon a maze and laid out like a map of the world with the books arranged by country of origin.

MR NORRELL'S LIBRARY AT HURTFEW ABBEY   Mr Gilbert Norrell's library in Susanna Clarke's *Jonathan Strange & Mr Norrell* (2004) contains England's finest collection of books on English magic. Mr Norrell studiously guards his precious books with a labyrinth spell, meaning that only those following Mr Norrell himself can find the entrance to the library. Those attempting to find the library alone are condemned to wander the seemingly endless corridors fruitlessly, only to keep returning to the same starting point.

LIBRARY TREASURES:
THE DIAMOND SUTRA

The Diamond Sutra (Or. 8210/p. 2) owned by the British Library is the earliest complete copy of a dated printed book in the world. The Diamond Sutra is a Buddhist religious text which was created in 868 CE. The text is in the form of a scroll over 5 metres long, made by pasting together seven strips of paper, on which the text had been printed using wooden blocks. Written in Chinese, the Diamond Sutra is one of the most important and sacred texts of the Buddhist faith; it is designed to be chanted and memorized so that it may be passed on (it is said to take 40 minutes to chant in full). Although older printed books exist, the Diamond Sutra is especially important because it has the date it was printed inscribed on the colophon. This copy was hidden, along with over 40,000 other ancient texts, in a blocked-up cave at a site known as the 'Caves of the Thousand Buddhas' near the Chinese city of Dunhuang in *c.* 1000 CE; thankfully, the dry desert climate allowed the books and manuscripts to survive. The secret cave was rediscovered and unblocked in 1900 by a monk named Wang Yuanlu. In 1907 the archaeologist and explorer Sir Marc Aurel Stein persuaded Wang Yuanlu to sell him a number of important ancient texts, including the Diamond Sutra. The significance of the book was not realized for some years, but today it is considered one of the chief treasures of the British Library.

LIBRARY SUPERLATIVES

Oldest library in the world The Library of Ashurbanipal, Nineveh, Assyria (now in Iraq) is thought to be one of the oldest libraries in the world. Established by Ashurbanipal, King of Assyria (668–c. 630 CE), the library was rediscovered by archaeologists in the 1850s. Over 30,000 cuneiform tablets and fragments containing historical and legal texts have been found; evidence suggests it was a systematically organized library.

Oldest working library The al-Qarawiyyin Library in Fez, Morocco, was founded in 859 by Fatima El-Fihriya, the daughter of a rich Tunisian merchant. El-Fihriya dedicated her life to establishing a mosque, university and library, and soon al-Qarawiyyin became a centre for Islamic culture. The library has remained continuously open to scholars since its inception and recently underwent a restoration, completed in 2016.

Oldest public library in the world The Biblioteca Malatestiana in Cesena, Italy, was founded in 1452 and is the world's oldest public library still housed in the original building, complete with original fittings (many books are still chained to the lecterns in medieval fashion).

Oldest public library in the English-speaking world Chetham's Library in Manchester was established in 1653 and is the oldest public library in England. Set up by the bequest of wealthy textile merchant Humphrey Chetham (1580–1653), the library was intended to be a free resource for scholars to rival the libraries of Oxford and Cambridge.

SMALLEST LIBRARY IN THE WORLD   While many phone-box and pop-up libraries have vied to be the smallest library in the world, the 'official' smallest library in the world according to the World Record Academy* is a library in Cardigan, Prince Edward Island, Canada. The tiny library measures just 3.5 × 3.5 metres and yet holds an impressive 1,800 books.

LARGEST LIBRARY IN THE WORLD   The Library of Congress in Washington DC is the world's largest library by size of collection, holding 162 million items in 838 miles of shelving. Some 12,000 items are added to the collection each day.

TALLEST LIBRARY IN THE WORLD   Shanghai Library in China is twenty-four storeys (106 metres) tall, making it the tallest library in the world.

LARGEST SINGLE-CHAMBER LIBRARY   The Long Room at Trinity College Dublin was built between 1712 and 1732 and is 65 metres long. The beautiful room contains two storeys of bookshelves running down each length. A stunning barrel ceiling was added in 1860 to add yet more space. The Long Room holds the library's 200,000 oldest books, which include the Book of Kells (*see page 91*).

---

* Guinness World Records do not have a category for the world's smallest library and therefore cannot verify the record.

MOST POPULAR LIBRARY
BOOK AUTHORS

Public Lending Right (PLR) collects statistics from UK libraries in order to ensure writers are paid for the loan of their books. The following list reveals the most popular authors in UK libraries in the first decade of the noughties (2000–2010).

AUTHOR	TIMES BOOKS LENT
1. Jacqueline Wilson	16 million
2. Danielle Steele	14 million
3. Catherine Cookson	14 million
4. Josephine Cox	13 million
5. James Patterson	11 million
6. R.L. Stine	10 million
7. Mick Inkpen	10 million
8. Janet and Allan Ahlberg	9 million
9. Roald Dahl	8 million
10. Agatha Christie	8 million

LEGAL DEPOSIT LIBRARIES

In 1610, Thomas Bodley, founder of Oxford's Bodleian Library, reached an agreement with the Stationers' Company of London that a copy of every book published in England would be deposited at his library. This agreement laid the foundations of the concept of legal deposit, which officially came into force in 1662.

Legal deposit required printers to supply the libraries of Oxford and Cambridge, in addition to the Royal Library (now the British Library), with a copy of every book published in the UK.* Legal deposit protects and preserves the output of the British publishing industry and ensures that national collections are constantly growing. Legal deposit was further reiterated under the first Copyright Act of 1710 and again in 1911. In 2003 and 2013 legal deposit was extended to include online and digital items such as websites, blogs, CD-ROMs and social media, ensuring libraries keep pace with technological innovation. The following libraries (with date they joined in parentheses) are the six legal deposit libraries in the UK:

Bodleian Library, Oxford (1662)
University Library Cambridge (1662)
The British Library (1709)[†]
National Library of Scotland (1709)[‡]
Trinity College Library, Dublin (1801)
National Library of Wales (1911)

---

* The British Library is the only library which nowadays automatically receives a copy of *every* book published in the UK or Ireland; the other libraries are entitled to *request* any book published within the previous twelve months.

† Previously the Royal Library.

‡ Previously the Advocates Library.

PUBLIC LENDING RIGHT

Public Lending Right (PLR) is a UK-wide scheme set up in 1979 to ensure writers, illustrators, translators and editors get paid when their books are taken out from public libraries. The PLR system is distinct from copyright and represents a recognition of an author's intellectual property rights. Authors are paid annually through government funds using a formula which calculates how many times their works were loaned by a library through a sample selection of library records – in 2014/15 the rate per loan was 7.67 pence up to a maximum payment of £6,600.* PLR tracks library loans throughout the UK. In 2014/15 the top ten most borrowed books were:

1. *Personal* by Lee Child
2. *Never Go Back* by Lee Child
3. *Abattoir Blues* by Peter Robinson
4. *The Silkworm* by Robert Galbraith†
5. *Invisible* by James Patterson
6. *Unlucky 13* by James Patterson
7. *Gone Girl* by Gillian Flynn
8. *Want You Dead* by Peter James
9. *Be Careful What You Wish For* by Jeffrey Archer
10. *Diary of a Wimpy Kid* by Jeff Kinney

---

* In 2016 only 219 of the 22,607 people eligible for PLR payments were paid the maximum amount of £6,600, whereas 17,718 earned nothing or less than £1.

† Pen name of J.K. Rowling.

FUTURE LIBRARY

In 2014, artist Katie Paterson created the Future Library, a project to collect 100 books by 100 writers from around the world over the course of 100 years. The books will be sealed unread in Oslo Library until 2114, when 3,000 copies of the works will be printed.

The first author to submit their work was the Canadian writer Margaret Atwood. In 2015 Atwood announced that her work was called *Scribbler Moon*, but no one knows if it is fiction, non-fiction, poetry, one word or 100,000 words long. In 2016 the second author to take part, David Mitchell, added his book, entitled *From Me Flows What You Call Time*, to the collection.

Each author must submit one digital and one hard copy of the work and promise not to tell anyone what their contribution is about, leaving them completely unread until 2114. Paterson has planted 1,000 trees in a forest in Nordmarka, Norway; it is from these trees in 2114 that the paper to print all the books in the project will come.

THE LIBRARY OF SMELLS

The Osmothèque (from the Greek *osme*, meaning odour, and *theke*, meaning storage) is a library of smells in Versailles, France. Founded in 1990, the Osmothèque is a repository for perfumes and contains over 3,200 scents, some 400 of which are no longer made. The collection is an archive of perfume-making history, and many fragrance houses and parfumiers have kindly donated samples of perfumes, both current and historical, in order to safeguard their formulas. The perfumes are stored in a special darkened room where they are kept at a constant temperature of 12°C with a protective layer of the inert gas argon. Some of the treasures of the collection are examples of extremely old perfumes, which cannot be found (or smelled) anywhere else, such as the fourteenth-century *L'Eau de la Reine de Hongrie* and *L'Eau de Cologne de Napoléon à Ste Hélène* from 1820. Although not open to the public, the Osmothèque holds a number of talks and workshops every year so that perfume fans can explore this unique collection.

CIRCULATING LIBRARIES

Before the advent of free public libraries those wishing to borrow books could join a circulating library. These enterprises were popular during the eighteenth and nineteenth centuries when few people could afford to buy large numbers of books and so turned to a circulating library from which, in return for a yearly subscription, books could be borrowed for a set period of time. Much as in modern libraries, members were fined if they were late returning a book. Circulating libraries were based in most large towns of the UK and had a mainly upper- and middle-class clientele, as the membership fees (of roughly 1 guinea a year for unlimited borrowing) were generally out of reach for an ordinary working-class family. The biggest circulating library during the eighteenth century was the Minerva Press Circulating Library in Leadenhall Street, London. It was founded by William Lane in the 1790s and was reported to have over 20,000 books.

It has been argued that circulating libraries were partly responsible for the growth in the popularity of fiction books during the Victorian period, as people who may not have considered buying a work of fiction could borrow one fairly cheaply. In the Victorian era Mudie's Select Library, which ran from 1842 to 1937, was famed for ensuring all the books it stocked were in line with the morals of the day. Many circulating libraries championed female writers and Gothic fiction. Such was their popularity that some branched out into publishing. However, after 1850 when free public libraries began to open and as the cost of books came down, circulating libraries were gradually squeezed out of the book market.

CHARLES DARWIN'S LIBRARY
ABOARD THE *BEAGLE*

Naturalist Charles Darwin spent five years (1831–36) aboard the *Beagle*, sailing around the world. It was during this voyage that he made a number of observations that would form the basis for his theory of natural selection. Darwin lived and worked in the library in the poop cabin at the stern of the ship, where some 400 volumes were available. Unfortunately the catalogue for the library was lost and on returning to England the collection was dispersed. However, in the 1980s the editors working on the *Correspondence of Charles Darwin* combed through Darwin's notebooks and letters to reconstruct a list of 132 books they thought were in his library. This was followed up in 2012–14 by Darwin Online, which continued the meticulous research to eventually create an online resource of the 180 works (or 404 volumes) which were probably part of Darwin's library aboard the *Beagle*. Below is listed a small selection of the books contained in Darwin's library.

- *Principles of Geology* (1830–33) by Charles Lyell
- *Personal Narrative of Travels to the Equinoctial Regions of America* (1819–29) by Alexander von Humboldt
- *A New Voyage and Description of the Isthmus of America* (1699) by Lionel Wafer
- *A New Voyage Round the World* (1697) by William Dampier

- *A Voyage to the Pacific Ocean* (1784) by James Cook
- *A Voyage Round the World* (1798–9) by Jean-François de Galaup de la Pérouse
- *Travels in South America* (1825) by Alexander Caldcleugh
- *Werner's Nomenclature of Colours** (1821) by Patrick Syme
- *Paradise Lost* by John Milton (1667)
- *A New General Atlas, Constructed from the Latest Authorities* (1823) by Aaron Arrowsmith
- *The Animal Kingdom Arranged in Conformity with its Organization* (1827–35) by Georges Cuvier

LIBRARY OF CONGRESS CLASSIFICATION SYSTEM

One of the most vital roles of a librarian or library is to catalogue and classify all the books in the library so as to allow the collection to be organized and searchable. A number of different systems to catalogue books (*see page 28*) have been developed over the years, but one of the most frequently used international standards is

---

* This wonderful book was like a pre-modern version of Pantone. Created for the use of taxonomic descriptions of plants and animals, it contained samples of many shades of named colours which scientists and naturalists in the field could use to label their work to ensure the true colours were re-created in later illustrations. Darwin frequently noted down the colour references from this book when making observations of new specimens.

that set up by the Library of Congress in Washington DC. The Library of Congress Classification system (LC) was developed in the late nineteenth and early twentieth centuries in order to organize and classify the collection of the Library of Congress, but was soon adopted by many other leading libraries, especially academic libraries.

The system is based on dividing all books into one of twenty-one subject headings, each of which is represented by a letter of the alphabet. Each subject heading is then further subdivided into further classifications, represented by one or two letters of the alphabet. For example, Law is classified under the letter K, and within this a further letter classification is given: thus KBM represents Jewish law, KBP Islamic law, and KBR the history of canon law. Within each subject classification, each area is further subdivided to represent the topic of a book: this can be classified by period, place or bibliographic form (periodicals, books, manuscripts etc.) and is represented by a number of one to four digits. For example, KBP469 represents the topic 'Influence of other legal systems on Islamic law'. This method of classifying books by subjects creates 'serendipitous browsing' whereby, because all books of a similar subject are shelved together, a reader may identify one work they need in the catalogue but then find many other useful related works right next to it on the shelf.

BOOK THEFTS

Ever since libraries have existed, unscrupulous types have stolen rare books and manuscripts from their reading rooms. In the Middle Ages librarians took to chaining the valuable books to desks to prevent theft, and today most rare-book rooms employ security guards. Some of the most audacious book thefts are detailed below.

In 2012 it was discovered that swathes of rare books had been stolen from Biblioteca Girolamini in Naples. Most shockingly it was revealed that the perpetrator was none other than the director of the library himself, Marino Massimo de Caro. The theft included rare works by Aristotle and Galileo. De Caro went to such lengths to cover his tracks that he defaced the catalogue card system and paid a forger to create fakes to substitute for the stolen originals. Just eighteen months after the thefts, Italian police reported that they had recovered almost 80 per cent of the stolen books.

The Vatican Library is home to a wealth of valuable manuscripts. Despite its careful security, a fourteenth-century copy of a Roman treatise on agriculture, which had been owned and annotated by the poet Petrarch, had a number of pages crudely cut out and stolen. Investigators were astounded to find that the beautifully illuminated pages had been stolen by an American scholar, Anthony Melnikas, who had used the library for over thirty years before going rogue and removing valuable pages which he later attempted to hawk to a rare-book dealer. Melnikas never admitted to stealing but was jailed for fourteen months in 1996 after pleading guilty to smuggling the stolen pages.

In 2006 map-dealer Edward Forbes Smiley III was caught attempting to steal rare maps from YALE UNIVERSITY LIBRARY after a librarian noticed he had dropped an X-Acto blade on the floor of the reading room. After his arrest Smiley admitted to stealing at least 97 rare maps worth over $3 million from six different institutions, including the British Library in London (although it is thought he may have stolen many more; the extent of his crimes may never be fully known). Smiley was sentenced to three and a half years in prison and ordered to pay back over $2 million in restitution.

Sweden's Royal Library, the KUNGLIGA BIBLIOTEKET, had over fifty-six valuable rare books, including Johannes Kepler's 1619 work *Harmonices Mundi* and Thomas Hobbes's 1651 *Leviathan*, stolen over a number of years. In 2004, it was discovered that the head of the library's manuscript department, Anders Burius, had been responsible for systematically stealing and selling rare works from the library for over ten years. Burius was arrested and questioned; he later committed suicide before many of the books could be found.

Dubbed the 'Tome Raider' by the media, William Jacques was Britain's most prolific book thief. Jacques was first caught in 2002 when he admitted to stealing and selling over 500 rare books worth over £1 million, including an Isaac Newton first edition which he stole from CAMBRIDGE UNIVERSITY LIBRARY and countless works from the LONDON LIBRARY. After fleeing to Cuba he later returned to Britain and was imprisoned for his crimes. On release he went on to steal at least thirteen rare books from the horticultural LINDLEY LIBRARY in London and was caught with a book hidden in his jacket and a list of seventy other works to pilfer. Jacques was sentenced to three and half years in prison and banned from every library in Britain.

LIGHTING A LIBRARY

Today we take it for granted that when we visit a library it will be brightly lit with electric lamps to allow us to consult the books of our choice with ease. However, back in earlier centuries when university libraries were first being constructed, architects needed to consider how to allow as much natural light in as possible in order to make the libraries useable spaces. Take, for example, the Bodleian Library in Oxford: when Sir Thomas Bodley opened the library in 1602 one of his most vehement statutes had been to ban 'fire or flame' from the library in order to protect the valuable books. This, however, meant that opening hours were severely limited to daylight, until artificial lights were finally installed throughout the library in 1929.

Traditionally medieval libraries had wooden lecterns instead of desks, at which the books were chained to prevent them from being stolen; windows would be positioned low to the ground to allow the light to illuminate the lecterns. After the invention of the printing press in the fifteenth century, when the cost of books reduced and as a result libraries grew massively in size, most of the old lecterns were stripped out and replaced by space-saving tall bookcases. This certainly allowed the expansion of the library but often to the cost of the daylight, as the high bookshelves limited the spread of the light around the room. Libraries newly built during this period (such as the Wren Library at Trinity College, Cambridge, which opened in 1695) reflect the need to increase the natural light flowing over the tall bookshelves with high ceilings and long, high windows.

In the nineteenth century artificial lighting began to be introduced in libraries as gas lamps provided relatively cheap, safe light. French architect Henri Labrouste (1801–1875) adopted this new technology and used it to inform the architecture for the reading rooms he designed in two libraries in Paris, the Bibliothèque nationale de France and the Bibliothèque Sainte-Geneviève. Labrouste used steel frames for the buildings (in part to negate the risk of fire posed by the use of gas lamps) to great effect, creating lofty ceilings, decorative cast-iron columns and large windows to let the light flow in. Labrouste's innovative use of cast-iron and gas lamps to increase light in libraries proved to be very influential: many new libraries in America followed his lead, most notably the Peabody Library in Baltimore, completed in 1878, which features a central atrium with a huge glazed roof encased by five storeys of book shelving, additionally lit with gas lamps.

Not everyone welcomed the era of the gas lamp. The British Museum's new round reading room, which opened in 1850, initially shunned artificial light and was lit by daylight alone; and many librarians began to raise questions about the safety of the gas lamps, noting that the fumes produced appeared to damage delicate books. By the late nineteenth century electric lighting had been developed and a number of institutions began experimenting with electric lights. In 1879, the British Museum installed a number of electric arc lamps in its reading room. As public libraries began opening, requiring longer opening hours, electric lights became more frequently installed in libraries. Today there is a move back towards increasing the use of natural light in modern libraries, with architects aiming to maximize the daylight in reading rooms, such as the stunning 'calendar of light' designed by Henning Larsen at Sweden's Malmö City Library, which utilizes a huge glass wall to help light the airy interior. Likewise the Beinecke Rare Book Library at Yale University, New Haven, was built with no windows; instead the exterior is honeycombed with sheets of translucent veined marble, which casts a delicate natural light into the interior of the library.

DEWEY DECIMAL
CLASSIFICATION SYSTEM

One of the oldest known general knowledge classification systems in the world, the Dewey Decimal Classification system (DDC) was developed by Melvil Dewey in 1873. It has been adopted by more than 200,000 libraries in 135 countries. The scheme works hierarchically by dividing knowledge into ten main subjects, meaning that books within the same subject group can be shelved together.* The ten main subject groupings are currently:

- 000   Computer Science, information and general works
- 100   Philosophy and psychology
- 200   Religion
- 300   Social sciences
- 400   Language
- 500   Science
- 600   Technology
- 700   Arts and recreation
- 800   Literature
- 900   History and geography

---

* It is said that prolific writer Isaac Asimov is the only person to have published books which have been represented in nine of the ten major Dewey Classification System categories; the only category he failed to produce a book in was '100 Philosophy'.

Each subject group is subdivided into ten subcategories (each represented by a number). For example, within the Science category are these ten subcategories:

500	Science
510	Mathematics
520	Astronomy
530	Physics
540	Chemistry
550	Earth sciences and geology
560	Fossils and prehistoric life
570	Biology
580	Plants (Botany)
590	Animals (Zoology)

These subcategories can then be further divided using the decimal system into ten more specific topics, and so on, meaning that the system can be constantly expanded to cover new subject classifications. A decimal point is used after the first three numbers to represent further specific topic subdivisions and make the number easier to read. The system is constantly reviewed, updated and revised by Forest Press, which oversees the system: the latest version was published in 2011 and is DDC23. Because the Dewey Classification system uses numbers, it serves as a common language among information professionals and has been translated into over thirty languages.

LIBRARY INSCRIPTIONS

Many libraries have mottoes or quotations inscribed on
their buildings to inspire readers. Below are samples
of the many library inscriptions.

'While men have wit to read and will to know,
the door to learning is the open book.'
BROOKLYN PUBLIC LIBRARY, NEW YORK

'Enlighten the people ... and tyranny and
oppressions of body and mind will vanish
like evil spirits at the dawn of day.'
UNIVERSITY LIBRARY AT RHODE ISLAND

'The inquiry, knowledge, and belief of truth is
the sovereign good of human nature.'
Bacon, Essays, 'Of Truth'
LIBRARY OF CONGRESS, WASHINGTON DC

QUOD FELICITER VORTAT ACADEMICI OXONIENS
BIBLIOTHECAM HANC VOBIS REIPUBLICAEQUE
LITERATORUM T.B.P
('That it might turn out happily, Oxonian academics,
for you and for the republic of lettered men
Thomas Bodley placed this library')
BODLEIAN LIBRARY, OXFORD

'Books alone are liberal and free
They give to all who ask
They emancipate all who serve them faithfully.'
LOS ANGELES PUBLIC LIBRARY

'Wisdom is the principal thing; therefore get wisdom: and with all thy getting get understanding.'
MANCHESTER CENTRAL LIBRARY

'The Commonwealth requires the education of the people as the safeguard of order and liberty.'
BOSTON PUBLIC LIBRARY

'The Library is the heart of the University.'
STERLING MEMORIAL LIBRARY
AT YALE UNIVERSITY

NUTRIMENTUM SPIRITUS ('Food for the soul')
BERLIN ROYAL LIBRARY

'Let there be light.'
EDINBURGH CENTRAL LIBRARY

MENS CUJUSQUE IS EST QUISQUE
('The mind is the man')
PEPYS LIBRARY, MAGDALENE COLLEGE,
CAMBRIDGE

THE NEW YORK PUBLIC LIBRARY LIONS

The pair of marble lions outside the magnificent Beaux-Arts New York Public Library on 5th Avenue and 42nd Street have become an iconic New York landmark. Sculptor Edward Clark Potter was paid $8,000 to model the lions and the Piccirilli family $5,000 to carve them from pink Tennessee marble (the same marble was used for Grand Central Station and the Lincoln Memorial). Since the library opened in 1911 the 6 foot by 12 foot lions have welcomed visitors into the library. Initially they were fondly nicknamed Leo Astor and Leo Lenox after the founders of the library, John Jacob Astor and James Lenox. But in the 1930s Mayor Fiorello LaGuardia suggested they be renamed to better represent the qualities New Yorkers would need to pull through the ongoing economic Depression, and since then they have been known as Patience and Fortitude (Patience is on the south side of the library steps, Fortitude on the north). Over the years the lions have frequently been decorated to celebrate the holidays or the success of local sports teams, but in 2004 the dressing-up was temporarily banned while they were steam-cleaned and restored to their former glory.

LIBRARY PHILANTHROPIST: ANDREW CARNEGIE

Andrew Carnegie was born in Dunfermline, Scotland, in 1835 and from lowly beginnings rose to become a hugely successful industrialist and one of the greatest ever library philanthropists. In 1848, due to economic hardship, the Carnegie family emigrated to Pennsylvania, USA. By the age of twelve Andrew was working as a bobbin boy in a cotton factory. Keen on self-improvement he read voraciously and attended night school. Carnegie was employed in a telegraph office before going to work at the Pennsylvania Railroad Company and rising rapidly through the ranks. He proved himself a shrewd investor and soon had a variety of business interests. During a business trip to Britain he met a number of steelworkers and saw the potential of a steel business in America, setting up what would become the very successful Carnegie Steel Company.

When Carnegie was sixty-five he decided to sell the company to J.P. Morgan for $480 million and retire to concentrate on philanthropic pursuits, of which he had many. He publicly stated that he believed the rich had a moral duty to use their wealth for the public good, and over the course of his life gave away over £350 million. Carnegie was especially interested in libraries and improving people's access to the means of self-education, but at this time very few public libraries existed. From 1883 to 1929 Carnegie used $56 million to build 2,509 libraries across the English-speaking world (including 1,689 in USA and 660 in the UK). His first library was built in his hometown of Dunfermline in 1883.

One of the many influential aspects of the Carnegie libraries was their early adoption of open stacks: this gave people direct access to the books on open shelves, making a library's collection more accessible than ever. Although a number of the original libraries have since been repurposed as public buildings, museums or offices, many hundreds survive today, still providing the free public library service Andrew Carnegie was so passionate about.

AUTHORS' LIBRARIES

Some libraries, such as the Harry Ransom Center at Texas University, specialize in collecting and preserving small libraries owned by authors. These book collections can give real insight into the inspiration behind famous writers. Authors' libraries in the Harry Ransom Center collection include:

VIRGINIA WOOLF   One hundred books from Virginia Woolf's personal library (the majority of Leonard and Virginia Woolf's personal library is kept at Washington State University Library). Seventy of the books in the collection are inscribed to Woolf herself, including works from T.S. Eliot, Lytton Strachey, E.M. Forster and Elizabeth Bowen. There are also a number of books which were re-bound by Woolf, including Ottoline Morrell's *A Farewell Message.*

EZRA POUND   Some 650 volumes from Ezra Pound's personal library were acquired from Pound's son Omar in 1980. At least thirty-eight of the books have been thoroughly annotated by Pound, revealing something of his thought process. An especial gem of Pound's collection is a first (American) edition of T.S. Eliot's *The Waste Land* (1922) inscribed to Pound.

EVELYN WAUGH   Waugh's personal library stretches to some 4,000 items and mainly includes works of nineteenth- and twentieth-century literature, plus books on art, gardening, design and architecture.

There are also a number of presentation copies of books dedicated to Waugh from fellow writers such as Graham Greene and Peter Quennell.

JAMES JOYCE   James Joyce's Trieste Library of 623 items was created by Joyce between 1900 and 1920. It contains copies of Joyce's own books signed by himself, books he used as sources for his own writing, and many signed and dedicated books from other authors.

ARTHUR CONAN DOYLE   The library has a selection of books (plus letters, papers and manuscripts) from Conan Doyle's True Crime and Spiritualism libraries.

JESSICA (DECCA) MITFORD   The library holds 166 books once owned by Jessica Mitford, the majority of which were used when she was writing and researching *Kind and Usual Punishment: The American Prison Business*.

LIBRARY FINES

Library fines are a way of encouraging readers to return overdue books and are used in libraries around the world. In many cases the fines do not accrue indefinitely, instead continuing to grow until a set point (for example, £5) is reached. Fines have been criticized for discouraging poorer readers from borrowing books, so instead many libraries use novel methods to pay off the fines, such as the marvellous 'Food for Fines' programme in which an amnesty on overdue books is declared and users may return late books as long as they donate some food to a food bank. According to the *Guinness Book of Records* the largest library fine ever paid was for the children's poetry book *Days and Deeds* by Burton E. Stevenson, which was taken out of the Kewanee Public Library in Kewanee, Illinois, in 1955 and not returned until forty-seven years later, accruing a fine of two cents per day, which came to a total of $345.14.

TOP TEN MOST BORROWED AUTHORS

According to Public Lending Right (PLR), which tracks library statistics across all UK libraries, the most popular authors in British libraries in 2014/15 were:

1. James Patterson
2. Julia Donaldson*
3. Daisy Meadows*
4. Francesca Simon*
5. M.C. Beaton
6. Adam Blade*†
7. Nora Roberts
8. Jacqueline Wilson*
9. Lee Child
10. Anna Jacobs

---

* Children's authors.

† The pseudonym used by the numerous authors who write the hugely successful Beast Quest and Sea Quest children's adventure stories for Working Partners.

THE VATICAN'S SECRET ARCHIVE

The Archivum Secretum Apostolicum Vaticanum or Vatican Secret Archive was created by Pope Paul V in 1612. It contains all the acts passed by the Holy See, plus papal correspondence, state papers and account books. The archive belongs to the reigning pope and when he dies it passes on to his successor. The use of the word 'secret' in the title derives from the old usage of the word meaning private or personal – relating to the fact that the archive is, in effect, the private archive of the papacy. The archives have been available to researchers since 1881 and today contain items accumulated in over 600 archival groups (the earliest of which is from the eighth century) on 53 miles of shelving. Some highlights of the collection are:

- The 1521 decree by Pope Leo X excommunicating Martin Luther.
- A 1530 petition signed and sealed by eighty-one English clergy and lords asking that Pope Clement VII annul the marriage of King Henry VIII and Katherine of Aragon.
- A copy of *Inter cetera*, the papal bull issued in 1493, the year after Christopher Columbus discovered America, effectively splitting the new continent between Spain and Portugal.
- Fourteenth-century transcripts from the trials of the Knights Templar, lasting for years after their arrests in 1307 by the French King Philip IV.

- A 1586 letter from Mary Queen of Scots to Pope Sixtus V. Written just months before she was executed, the letter reaffirms her Catholic faith and implores the Pope to intercede on her behalf.
- Papers relating to the seventeenth-century Vatican trial for heresy of Galileo Galilei.
- A 1650 letter written on silk to Pope Innocent X by Chinese Empress Dowager Wang, who had converted to Catholicism.

NATIONAL LIBRARIES

The principle of a national library originated in royal collections of books and manuscripts, which established the idea that a nation's intellectual output should be preserved for posterity. The first official national library was that housed at the British Museum in London, which was established in 1753 and later became the basis for the British Library. This library was to be a national resource, rather than a collection held by the monarch or Church, and was to be freely available to the public. However, due to the nature of a national library with its aims to collect and protect rare and valuable books and to secure copies of the nation's publishing output through legal deposit (*see page 14*), most national libraries do not lend books, but rather allow readers to consult the collection within their reading rooms. Some national libraries of note and the year of their creation are listed below.

NAME	LOCATION	EST.
The British Library	London	1753/1973*
Bibliothèque nationale de France	Paris	1792
US Library of Congress	Washington DC	1800
National Library of Russia	St Petersburg	1795
German National Library	Leipzig	1913
National Library of Australia	Canberra	1960
National Library of Brazil	Rio de Janeiro	1810
National Library of China	Beijing	1909
National Library of India	Calcutta	1953
National Library of Ireland	Dublin	1877
National Central Library of Florence	Florence†	1714
National Diet Library	Tokyo	1948
Egyptian National Library & Archives	Cairo	1870
National Library of Scotland	Edinburgh	1925
National Library of Wales	Aberystwyth	1907

---

* The Department of Printed Books was established at the British Museum 1753; in 1973 a new national library was created and the collection amalgamated.

† Italy actually has nine national libraries, including two central national libraries: one in Florence, and another smaller one in Rome.

ERNEST SHACKLETON'S LIBRARY
ABOARD THE *ENDURANCE*

When Sir Ernest Shackleton set off on his expedition
to the South Pole in 1914 he made sure to stock the
shelves of his cabin aboard the *Endurance* with plenty of
good reading material.* In January 1915 the *Endurance*
became stuck in the ice of the Weddell Sea, marking
the start of an epic struggle for Shackleton and his
crew to survive and escape across the ice to safety.†
The *Endurance*, stranded in the ice for many months,
was ultimately abandoned and left to sink. Historians
were thus unaware of the contents of Shackleton's
library. However, in 2016 an image of Shackleton's
cabin taken in 1915, picturing the many books on his
shelf, was digitized, finally allowing historians the
opportunity to decipher the books in the *Endurance*'s
library. Shackleton's library revealed a combination of
reference books, accounts of exploration, along with
modern and classic novels.

---

* Shackleton was a bibliophile: during his previous trip to the Antarctic
for the Nimrod Expedition of 1907–09 he took a printing press in order to
fill the many long hours. Shackleton therefore became the first person to
publish a book on Antarctica, where he bound and printed *Aurora australis*,
in 1909, using wooden boards fashioned from a tea chest.

† The *Endurance* was stranded in pack ice over the Antarctic winter of
1915, drifting with the moving ice. The 28-man crew eventually abandoned
ship and camped on the inhospitable ice before taking the lifeboats and
sailing to the uninhabited and remote Elephant Island. Desperate for rescue,
Shackleton and five of his crew then set off in an open boat on the perilous
800-mile trip to South Georgia, from where, at last, a rescue party could
be dispatched to collect the remaining crew on Elephant Island. Remark-
ably all twenty-eight men survived the ordeal and returned home safely.

- *Pros and Cons: A Newspaper Reader's and Debater's Guide to the Leading Controversies of the Day* by J.B. Askew (1896)
- *The Northwest Passage* by Roald Amundsen (1908)
- *The Voyage of the Fox in the Arctic Seas* by Francis Leopold McClintock (1859)
- *The Brothers Karamazov* by Fyodor Dostoyevsky (1880)
- *Encyclopedia Britannica*
- *The Case of Miss Elliott* by Emmuska Orczy (1905)
- *Almayer's Folly* by Joseph Conrad (1895)
- *The Concise Oxford Dictionary*
- *The Threshold of the Unknown Region* by Clements Markham (1873)
- *Narrative of a Voyage to the Polar Sea during 1875–6* by George Nares (1878)
- *Potash and Perlmutter* by Montague Glass (1910)
- *Cassell's Book of Quotations* by William Gurney Benham

HERBARIA

A herbarium is a library of plant samples in which preserved plants are stored and catalogued to allow botanists and taxonomists to identify plants, find out when they flower, where they can be found and what their official name is. Each plant in the collection should include a sample of the bark, leaves, stem and flower or fruit plus a drawing or photograph and, in more modern collections, a sample of the plant's DNA. Many of the plants in the collection will have been pressed and dried, a system for preserving plants that has been in use for hundreds of years and remains one of the best ways to preserve the form and colour of a plant. There are over 3,000 herbaria around the world, many of which specialize in different plant species. For example, the Herbarium at Kew Gardens has a special collection of ferns and fungi; the Herbaria at the Natural History Museum in London specialize in seaweed; and the New York Botanical Gardens Herbarium has a particular emphasis on New World plants. The oldest (and largest, with over 8 million plant samples) herbarium in the world is at the Muséum national d'histoire naturelle in Paris, which was established in 1635.

THE MAGICIANS' LIBRARY

The Conjuring Arts Research Center was established in 2003 in Manhattan, New York. A non-profit organization, its primary role is as a library for books on magic and related arts such as hypnosis, ventriloquism, juggling and sleight of hand. The library currently holds over 12,000 books on magic in numerous different languages and includes rare texts from the fifteenth century. The collection is especially strong on early magic, holding over five hundred books on magic printed before 1700. As well as books the library holds a number of magic periodicals, has an extensive collection of manuscripts featuring magic methods, and holds some 20,000 items of correspondence between magicians, including the great 'cardician' Ed Marlo (1913–1991). The centre is open to the public but those wishing to peruse the collection must make an appointment.

LIBRARY TREASURES: THE HAMBURG BIBLE

The Hamburg Bible (also known as the Bible of Bertoldus) (MS. GKS 4 2°) is a lavishly illustrated Bible created for Hamburg Cathedral in 1255. The unique Bible is in three huge volumes and includes exceptional illuminated letters, providing an invaluable source of medieval art. The Bible contains eighty-nine beautifully illuminated initials following the themes of biblical books, with one section including images of the process of medieval book production. The manuscript was purchased by the Royal Library in Copenhagen, Denmark, in 1784. Due to its immense value as a source on the craft of the book in Europe in the medieval period it was inscribed into the UNESCO Memory of the World register in 2011.

LIBRARY HAND

'Library hand' was a specific rounded style of cursive script that was developed to standardize handwriting, and was taught in schools for librarians from the nineteenth century into the mid-twentieth century. A handbook produced by the New York State School for Librarians in 1916 had this to say of the importance of a good library hand:

> At first thought it seems as if emphasizing a merely mechanical accomplishment as an important qualification for library work were subordinating the intellectual side and setting up a fictitious and finical standard. Whatever the theory, the fact remains that nothing pays the candidate for a library position better for the time it costs than to be able to write a satisfactory library hand.

During the period when library catalogues were filed on index cards (*see page 97*) legibility was of extreme importance and it was thought useful for all librarians to share a standard handwriting. Many different examples of library hand were developed in different institutions, but one of the key trailblazers was Melvil Dewey, the librarian who developed Dewey Decimal Classification (*see page 28*). Writing in 1887 in *Library Notes: Improved Methods and Labor-savers for Librarians, Readers and Writers* Dewey set out the specifications for his library hand.

a. Size. Hight [*sic*] of m one space or 5–12 the distance between standard 6 mm rulings of catalog card. Hight of b, f, h, k, l, two spaces. Hight of d, p, t, 1¾ space, f, g, j, y, z, extend a full space, and p, q, ¾ space below the line.

b. Figures all 1½ spaces high except 6, 7, and 9, two spaces.

c. Capitals extend two spaces above the line, and J also runs a full space below.

d. No shading. Uniform *black* line. Avoid fine strokes.

e. Letters upright, with as little slant as possible and that a trifle backward rather than forward, and uniformly the same.

f. Join the letters of a word so as to make one word picture.

g. Separate words by space of an m, and sentences by two m's.

h. Uniformity. Take great pains to have all writing uniform in size, blackness of lines, slant, spacing and forms of letters.

i. Use only standard library ink, and let it dry without blotting.

j. Follow the library hand forms for all letters, avoiding any ornament, flourish, or lines not necessary to the letter.

At Cambridge University Library, Alwyn Faber Scholfield, the librarian from 1923 to 1949, produced a number of index cards with his library hand on which all new recruits were required to copy until they could produce exact replicas, ensuring that entries in the catalogue all looked the same.* The rise of the typewriter in the early twentieth century and the use of computerized cataloguing systems negated the need for a standard library hand and the practice died out.

ART LIBRARIES

Libraries are not just depositories for books and manuscripts; some specialize in a different form. Around the world there are numerous art libraries which collect and curate items from the art world, from sculpture to fashion. Art libraries of note include the following.

The NATIONAL ART LIBRARY in the Victoria & Albert Museum in London is a national resource of fine and decorative arts. There are over 1 million items in the collection including photos, prints, drawings, paintings, textiles, furniture, sculpture, glassware, ceramics and fashion. The library also specializes in the art of book design, so the collection includes many early printed books and fine bindings.

The RIJKSMUSEUM LIBRARY is part of the Dutch National Museum in Amsterdam. It has a collection of over 350,000 items relating to the history of art. The collection focuses on the history of painting,

---

* Scholfield used the traditional 'The quick brown fox jumped over the lazy dogs' as well as the more unusual 'The judge spoke most finely but with very quixotic zeal'.

printmaking and sculpture in Western Europe from the Middle Ages to the twentieth century. The Library also holds some fascinating special collections, including over 60,000 art auction catalogues from 1722 to 1932.

The AVERY ARCHITECTURAL AND FINE ARTS LIBRARY is part of Columbia University in New York; it is the largest architecture library in the world. The Library owns a copy of the first Western printed book on architecture, *De re aedificatoria* (*Ten Books on Architecture*) by Leone Battista Alberti (1485), and holds the archive of Frank Lloyd Wright.

The MUSEUM OF MODERN ART LIBRARY in New York holds a substantial collection of items associated with modern and contemporary art from 1800 to the present day. The collection includes ephemera relating to modern artists, plus visual art, photography, design, performance and emerging art forms.

ST BRIDE LIBRARY in London is the foremost library in the world devoted to graphic arts and printing. It holds a collection of over 60,000 items connected to the printing trade, including printing type from Oxford University Press, the archives of typographer Eric Gill and 10,000 specimens of British type.

The BRITISH FILM INSTITUTE'S NATIONAL ARCHIVE is one of the largest and most important film libraries in the world. Established in 1935, the Archive holds over 275,000 feature and short films plus over 210,000 television programmes. One of the key roles of the archive is to preserve and restore delicate early films.

The IRENE LEWISOHN COSTUME REFERENCE LIBRARY at New York's Metropolitan Museum of Art is one of the best fashion libraries in the world. The Library is primarily for the use of curators at the museum's Costume Institute, but occasionally scholars are allowed access to the vast collection of 25,000 books and periodicals and 1,500 designer files relating to the history of fashion and costume.

THE BRITISH MUSEUM READING ROOM

Before the purpose-built building in St Pancras was opened in 1997, the main British Library reading room was at the British Museum. Designed by Sydney Smirke, the beautiful round room is situated in the centre of the museum's courtyard. Construction started in 1854 and Smirke used cast iron, glass and concrete to create a beautiful domed space, purportedly based on the Pantheon in Rome. The ceiling is made of papier mâché and painted in pale blue, cream and gold.* The reading room opened in 1857 with 3 miles of bookcases (and 25 miles of shelving) around

---

* When the room was first opened the Keeper of Manuscripts Sir Frederic Madden was unimpressed by the ornamentation, commenting that the reading room was 'a gilded dome ... utterly unfitted for the real purpose of study'.

the 46.2 metre diameter. To use the reading room researchers had to apply in writing to the principal librarian. Famous names who were issued with a reader's ticket include:

Bram Stoker | Karl Marx | Thomas Hardy
Sir Arthur Conan Doyle | Vladimir Lenin*
Rudyard Kipling | Charles Dickens| George Orwell
Mahatma Gandhi | Virginia Woolf

The bookstacks were moved to the British Library in St Pancras in 1997 and the room underwent significant restoration. In 2000 it reopened and all museum visitors could enter the reading room for the first time. Between 2007 and 2013 the reading room was used as an exhibition space but is currently closed while the museum consults on its future.

LIBRARY PHILANTHROPIST: J.P. MORGAN

John Pierpont (J.P.) Morgan (1837–1913) was born into a wealthy banking family and followed his father into the business. Morgan was a very successful entrepreneur, ultimately buying up and reorganizing much of the American railroad system, consolidating various electricity companies to create General Electric, and

---

* Under the name Jacob Richter.

taking a role in the creation of the United States Steel Corporation. These many and varied business interests allowed Morgan to wield a lot of power and influence over America's financial markets in an era before the existence of central banks. In 1907 Morgan was instrumental in mitigating the effects of a serious financial crisis, organizing bailouts and stabilizing the markets: although successful, this did cause many to worry about one individual holding so much power over the American economy.

Morgan was a passionate collector of art, books and gems; many of his collections have been donated to public museums such as the Metropolitan Museum of Art in New York. In 1906 the Morgan Library and Museum (then known as the Pierpont Morgan Library) was founded in New York to house his extensive book collection. In 1924 Morgan's son, John Pierpont Morgan Jr, made the library a public institution in accordance with the wishes of his father. The eclectic collection holds treasures such as three Gutenberg Bibles, a number of spectacular illuminated manuscripts, one of Charles Dickens's manuscripts for *A Christmas Carol*, Beethoven's annotated scores, Walter Scott's original manuscript for *Ivanhoe*, and a scrap of paper on which Bob Dylan wrote the lyrics for 'Blowin' in the Wind'.

LIBRARY OF CONGRESS,
WASHINGTON DC

President John Adams signed the Library of Congress into being in April 1800 when he approved legislation for the creation of a library for the use of Congress in the new capital of Washington DC, granting $5,000 for 'such books as may be necessary for the use of Congress – and for putting up a suitable apartment for containing them therein'. The first books to furnish the library were ordered from London and arrived in 1801; by 1802 the library had its first catalogue, which listed some 964 items and 9 maps.

Unfortunately in 1814 the British invaded the Capitol and burnt down the library, which by that time contained some 3,000 items. Former president Thomas Jefferson was keen to see the valuable library restocked and so sold his own private collection to Congress for $23,950 in order to begin again. Jefferson's impressive book collection totalled 6,487 volumes and provided the basis for a wide-ranging Library for Congress encompassing books in many subjects and languages. Sadly in 1851 a fire took hold in the library, destroying roughly two-thirds of the 55,000 items in the collection, many of which were subsequently replaced by generous benefactors.

By 1870 a copyright law requiring two copies of all books published in America to be sent to the Library of Congress was passed, ensuring the collection was constantly growing and enshrining the Library of

Congress as a national library. In 1897 a huge new Renaissance-style library building designed by John L. Smithmeyer and Paul J. Pelz was opened. Today the Library of Congress is the largest library in the world (*see page 4*), holding over 162 million items, including 17 million catalogued books.

PRESIDENTIAL LIBRARIES

In 1941 President Franklin D. Roosevelt became the first US president to establish his library as an official repository for all his books, archives and items relating to his presidency. Since then every American president has nominated a library to document their legacy. In 1955 the Presidential Libraries Act made the creation of a presidential library law. There are thirteen presidential libraries across America.[*]

PRESIDENT	TERM	LOCATION
Herbert Hoover	1929–33[†]	West Branch, Iowa
Franklin D. Roosevelt	1933–45	Hyde Park, New York
Harry S. Truman	1945–53	Independence, Missouri
Dwight D. Eisenhower	1953–61	Abilene, Kansas

[*] Barack Obama's library is expected to be completed by 2020.
[†] Hoover's library was not dedicated until 1962.

John F. Kennedy	1961–63	Boston, Massachusetts
Lyndon B. Johnson	1963–69	Austin, Texas
Richard Nixon	1969–74	Yorba Linda, California
Gerald R. Ford	1974–77	Ann Arbor, Michigan
Jimmy Carter	1977–81	Atlanta, Georgia
Ronald Reagan	1981–89	Simi Valley, California*
George H.W. Bush	1989–93	College Station, Texas
William J. Clinton	1993–2001	Little Rock, Arkansas
George W. Bush	2001–09	Dallas, Texas
Barack Obama	2009–17	Chicago

MOBILE LIBRARIES

Mobile libraries were first introduced to help people living in an area without a library to get access to books. The earliest mobile libraries were horse-drawn carts – one of the first in Britain appeared in 1857, created by Victorian philanthropist George Moore; it involved a perambulating library operating in a circle of eight villages across Cumbria. Another early mobile library was the Warrington Perambulating Library, which was organized by the Warrington Mechanics' Institute in 1858. In 1905 a mobile library service was

---

* The original Air Force One, which flew for twenty-nine years and served seven presidents, is on display at Reagan's presidential library.

instigated in Washington County after the librarian at the Washington County Free Library realized their service was not reaching those out in remote rural areas. A book wagon was established to take books from the library out to people living rurally who otherwise would not have access to the collection.

The first motorized mobile library in Britain came in the form of a Ford van with shelving for up to 900 books and was introduced in the 1920s in Perthshire, Scotland. Mobile libraries are still going strong around the world, with many modes of transport used to distribute books, from camels in Kenya, library ships in western Norway, an elephant library in Thailand, and Books on Bikes run by the Seattle Public Library.

BOOK STORAGE

The development of the library has gone hand in hand with the development of book storage – what is a library, after all, if not a repository for books? The first libraries were filled with manuscripts in the shape of scrolls. The Royal Library of Alexandria, for example, was estimated to have had up to 700,000 parchment scrolls, which were stored in labelled armaria – specially built closed wooden cupboards. Armaria were used to store scrolls up until the Middle Ages; it is thought that the scrolls were stacked lengthways, with an identification tag attached to the side of the scroll, making them easier to find. In Greek libraries there was a room for storing scrolls and a separate room for reading, whereas in a Roman library the scrolls would be stored and read in the same space.

From the second century CE codices were developed, changing the shape (quite literally) of book storage. Manuscripts in codex form might be stored in chests or on shelves, or later chained on lecterns. In medieval monasteries, the manuscripts might be stored in library rooms, but the monks and scribes would copy and read their books in the cloister, in carrels – individual desks with high sides (today often seen in university libraries) to isolate the reader from distractions. Some sixteenth-century engravings have furnished us with images of the innovative book wheel – a large rotating wooden wheel, rather like a waterwheel in appearance, holding between three and six volumes; the reader sits at the base of the wheel and turns it to access the next book.

The library built at Oxford University by 1488 originally stored the manuscripts given by Duke Humfrey of Gloucester (d. 1447) on wooden lecterns. When Sir Thomas Bodley refurbished and reopened Duke Humfrey's Library in 1602, his replacement folio volumes were kept chained on new-style bookshelves which replaced the old lecterns. When in 1612 an extension, known as Arts End, was added to Duke Humfrey's Library it was the first library in England to include a new method for storing books – bookshelves running from floor to ceiling with a gallery to allow access to the upper part of the shelves.

With the advent of the printing press, books became much cheaper and library collections grew exponentially: storing books vertically in bookshelves became the most space-efficient method.

TOP TEN MOST BORROWED AUDIOBOOKS

Audiobooks have grown in popularity in the last few years. Public Lending Right (PLR), which pays authors, illustrators, translators and editors for every work taken out of a library in the UK, included audiobooks in its calculation for the first time in 2014/15.

The top ten most popular audiobooks taken out from British libraries in 2014/15 were:

1. *Without a Trace* by Lesley Pearse,
   read by Emma Powell
2. *Harry Potter and the Philosopher's Stone*
   by J.K. Rowling, read by Stephen Fry
3. *Harry Potter and the Deathly Hallows*
   by J.K. Rowling, read by Stephen Fry
4. *Demon Dentist* by David Walliams,
   read by David Walliams[*]
5. *The Cuckoo's Calling* by Robert Galbraith,
   read by Robert Glenister

---

[*] Two separate editions of the same book, counted separately.

6. *Demon Dentist* by David Walliams,
   read by David Walliams[*]
7. *The Silkworm* by Robert Galbraith,
   read by Robert Glenister
8. *Never Go Back* by Lee Child, read by Jeff Harding
9. *Be Careful What You Wish For* by Jeffrey Archer,
   read by Alex Jennings
10. *Ratburger* by David Walliams,
    read by David Walliams

MOST CHALLENGED LIBRARY BOOKS IN AMERICA

The American Library Association (ALA) keeps a record of all the books that are challenged or banned in libraries and schools across America. The ALA does not ban books itself but publicizes the practice to highlight the pernicious effect of censorship on libraries. Over the years the books that are most often challenged are those with a sexual element or books which use obscene language: many of those seeking to ban books do so to try to 'protect' children from content they see as unsuitable. The ALA's policy on censorship states that 'Librarians and governing bodies should maintain that parents – and only parents – have the right and the responsibility to restrict the access of their children – and only their children – to library resources.'

In 2015 the most challenged book was *Looking for Alaska* by John Green. In the first decade of this century (2000–2009) the top ten most challenged books in American libraries were:

1. *Harry Potter* (series) by J.K. Rowling
2. *Alice* (series) by Phyllis Reynolds Naylor
3. *The Chocolate War* by Robert Cormier
4. *And Tango Makes Three* by Justin Richardson and Peter Parnell
5. *Of Mice and Men* by John Steinbeck
6. *I Know Why the Caged Bird Sings* by Maya Angelou
7. *Scary Stories* (series) by Alvin Schwartz
8. *His Dark Materials* (series) by Philip Pullman
9. *ttyl*; *ttfn*; *l8r g8r* (series) by Lauren Myracle
10. *The Perks of Being a Wallflower* by Stephen Chbosky

The top ten most challenged books 1990–99 were:

1. *Scary Stories* (series) by Alvin Schwartz
2. *Daddy's Roommate* by Michael Willhoite
3. *I Know Why the Caged Bird Sings* by Maya Angelou
4. *The Chocolate War* by Robert Cormier
5. *The Adventures of Huckleberry Finn* by Mark Twain
6. *Of Mice and Men* by John Steinbeck
7. *Forever* by Judy Blume
8. *Bridge to Terabithia* by Katherine Paterson
9. *Heather Has Two Mommies* by Lesléa Newman
10. *The Catcher in the Rye* by J.D. Salinger

WRITERS' ARCHIVES

In recent years scholars have become especially interested in how famous writers worked and what their influences were. To this end many libraries now hold the archives of writers, which include correspondence, notes, works in progress, original manuscripts and, sometimes, personal items such as photographs or diaries. Below is a list of famous writers and the libraries which hold their papers.*

WRITER	LIBRARY
F. Scott Fitzgerald	Princeton University Library
Jack Kerouac	New York Public Library
Virginia Woolf	British Library
Shelley–Godwin†	Bodleian Library, Oxford
George Eliot	New York Public Library
Charles Darwin	Cambridge University Library
Sylvia Plath	Lilly Library, Indiana University, Bloomington
Victor Hugo	John Rylands Library, Manchester
Gabriel García Márquez	Harry Ransom Center, Texas University
George Orwell	University College London Library

---

  * Note that not all papers relating to each writer are held at one location, so the institutions listed are a major holder of that author's work but probably not the only one.

  † The archive holds the papers of Percy Bysshe Shelley, his wife Mary Shelley plus her parents Mary Wollstonecraft and William Godwin.

ENEMIES OF THE LIBRARY

Ever since libraries have existed wily librarians have needed to protect their collection from a variety of threats, many of which persist to this day.

VANDALS   Books are very vulnerable to theft (*see page 23*) or vandalism, and so most libraries with a valuable collection restrict access to their collection, employ guards to keep an eye on readers and ban pens from reading rooms.

PESTS   Rodents, birds and insects* can all cause damage to a book collection. Libraries may use sticky traps to identify enemy insects, and acquisitions of old books may have to be quarantined to ensure against infestations. Much insect damage in old books is blamed on the legendary bookworm; however, no single species can be defined as a bookworm as many beasties like to eat through starchy old paper. The most common culprits for 'bookworm' infestation are silverfish (*Thysanura*) and paperlouse (*Psocoptera*).

LIGHT   Anyone who has left a newspaper in direct sunlight for a couple of days will notice how quickly the paper is coloured and degraded by exposure to bright light. Ultraviolet light is the most damaging: to protect collections windows may be covered with UV filters, and especially fragile items may be stored in boxes.

---

* At the Rococo Library in Portugal's Mafra National Palace, a colony of bats is allowed to reside in the library to eat the book-damaging bugs.

HUMIDITY AND TEMPERATURE   High temperatures and humidity often go hand in hand, and both can speed the degradation of books and encourage mould and insects. Fluctuations in temperature are also harmful, so it is suggested that heat and humidity levels are controlled and maintained at a constant level.[*]

FIRE   Libraries are at a great risk from fire and most modern libraries will carry out extensive fireproofing, such as maintaining a low-oxygen environment. Prospective readers at the Bodleian are still required to promise 'not to bring into the Library or kindle therein any fire or flame'.

FLOOD   Water[†] can be as damaging as fire, and collections have been damaged by flooding or overzealous use of sprinkler systems to put out fires. Books can be dried out using dehumidifiers or, if severely damaged, by conservation specialists.

POLLUTION   Pollution from busy roads or nearby industrial sites can be counteracted by using window and door seals and employing air-filtration systems. Additionally items should be stored in modern archival boxes, which will minimize exposure to pollutants.

----

[*] British Standard BSI PD 5454 outlines best practice for the storage of archive materials: it is recommended that the temperature is kept between 13°c and 20°c and relative humidity at 35–60 per cent.

[†] In 1673 a valuable collection of books was moved from Yorkshire to the Bodleian Library in Oxford, but unfortunately it was transported in torrential rain and suffered significant water damage. In an early feat of conservation, antiquarian Anthony Wood laid the books out to dry on the lead roof of the picture gallery.

BOOK FORMATS

Today libraries are filled with bookshelves hosting miles and miles of books, but libraries have not always stored material in the form of a book. Other more ancient formats were previously more common in libraries; in the future it seems likely that digital storage of e-books may become the norm. Below is a short round-up of book formats over time.

CLAY, WOODEN OR WAX TABLETS   The Sumerians created cuneiform, one of the earliest forms of writing, in *c.* 3000 CE, which they marked onto clay tablets with a wedge-shaped stylus. These tablets were used to record laws, accounts and literature and were stored in libraries. The Ancient Greeks and Romans used a folded pair of wooden tablets filled with wax to create a surface which could be written on and reused. These wax tablets were generally used for more ephemeral uses such as recording business transactions, whereas literature would have more likely been recorded on scrolls.

ANCIENT SCROLLS   Many ancient writings were recorded on a scroll – a roll of paper, parchment or papyrus. Scrolls are often rolled with wooden rollers, which allow the reader to unroll the text, one section or page at a time. Scrolls originated in the Eastern Mediterranean, Egypt and Middle East and were used throughout the ancient world until superseded by the codex.

CODEX   Developed in the second or third century
CE by the Romans, the codex was a precursor to the
modern book, made from pages of papyrus stitched
together between wooden boards. Initially codices
were mostly used for note-taking or technical works,
but as printing developed they became a popular way
of producing Bibles. This new shape of 'book' completely changed the way libraries stored and displayed
material (*see page 54*). At first codices were stacked
any which way, and sometimes with the spine facing
inwards towards the shelf; this made it hard to identify
the books, so to mitigate this a design was occasionally
embossed on the fore-edge of the pages. The first
book with a printed spine was produced in *c.* 1535;
this development standardized the way books were
displayed – stacked vertically with their spines facing
out.

PARCHMENT MANUSCRIPTS   Pre-Gutenberg, most
books were created by hand by monks working in a
scriptorium. From about the fifth century CE, monks
copied out texts onto parchment. In the medieval
period manuscripts would be lavishly decorated with
illuminated letters and illustrations.

PRINTED BOOKS   From the 1450s, when Johannes
Gutenberg invented the printing press, the production
of books went from taking many months of painstaking
work by many hands to being produced relatively
quickly and cheaply by a machine. This development
was a giant leap forwards for the technology of the

book and massively increased the volume of books on the market and, therefore, in libraries. Today books are printed in hardback or paperback editions and are of fairly standardized sizes.

DIGITAL   Electronic books or e-books were developed in 1971 by Project Gutenberg, a project to create an open access digital library. Thanks to the prevalence of tablets and e-readers, e-books are booming and many libraries are now starting to store and lend more books digitally, with some choosing to go exclusively digital. Storing books digitally on servers takes up a lot less space in a library and, as more ancient books are digitized, allows more public access to our literary treasures.

THE BRITISH LIBRARY

The British Library is surprisingly modern as national libraries go, only officially coming into being through an Act of Parliament in 1973. To create a British national library a number of libraries were merged:

The British Museum Library
National Central Library
National Lending Library for Science and Technology
British National Bibliography Office
for Scientific and Technical Information
India Office Library and Records
British Institute of Recorded Sound

Initially the holdings were dotted in various locations around London and the UK, until a new purpose-built library was opened at St Pancras in 1997. The library building was the largest public building to have been constructed in the UK in the twentieth century; it was designed by British architect Colin St John Wilson.

The foundation of the collection was that of the British Museum, which was established in 1753 and was a legal deposit library (*see page 14*), taking in a copy of every work published in the UK. This extensive collection included the 'foundation collections' of Sir Hans Sloane, Sir Robert Cotton and Robert Harley (*see page 123*), together with King George II's Old Royal Library and King George III's King's Library, as created in the seventeenth and eighteenth centuries. Today the collection represents the world's second largest library collection; it is split between St Pancras with its reading rooms and the huge document and newspaper storage site at Boston Spa in Yorkshire, which has space for 7 million items.

THE LIBRARY IN QUOTATIONS

'A public library is the most enduring of
memorials, the trustiest monument for the
preservation of an event or a name or an
affection; for it, and it only, is respected by
wars and revolutions, and survives them.'
Mark Twain (1835–1910)

'I ransack public libraries and find them
full of sunken treasure.'
Virginia Woolf (1882–1941)

'We may sit in our library and yet
be in all quarters of the earth.'
John Lubbock (1834–1913)

'If you have a garden and a library,
you have everything you need.'
Cicero (106–43 BCE)

'There is not such a cradle of democracy upon
the earth as the Free Public Library, this
republic of letters, where neither rank, office,
nor wealth receives the slightest consideration.'
Andrew Carnegie (1835–1919)

'The student has his Rome, his Florence, his
whole glowing Italy, within the four walls of
his library. He has in his books the ruins of an
antique world and the glories of a modern one.'
Henry Wadsworth Longfellow (1807–1882)

'Books constitute capital. A library book lasts as long as a house, for hundreds of years. It is not, then, an article of mere consumption but fairly of capital, and often in the case of professional men, setting out in life, it is their only capital.'
Thomas Jefferson (1743–1826)

SOME FAMOUS LIBRARIANS OF NOTE

MAO ZEDONG (1893–1976)   Mao was assistant librarian at Peking University 1918–19 before becoming involved in politics. Mao's time at the library had a huge influence on him, as he worked under chief librarian Li Dazhao, who went on to co-found the Chinese Communist Party.

JACOB GRIMM (1785–1863)   Jacob Grimm worked as a librarian to support himself while following his life's passion – researching and collecting traditional fairy stories with his brother Wilhelm. At one point Jacob worked as private librarian to the King of Westphalia and later went on to work at the University of Göttingen.

PHILIP LARKIN (1922–1985)   Throughout his writing career Larkin worked as a librarian, serving for thirty years at the Brynmor Jones Library at the University of Hull.

J. Edgar Hoover (1895–1972)   Before becoming the head honcho at the FBI, Hoover worked at the Library of Congress as a cataloguer. What Hoover learnt at the Library of Congress was later to inspire the creation of his legendary filing system for FBI files.

David Hume (1711–1776)   While working on his famous six-volume work *The History of England*, philosopher David Hume worked as a librarian at the Advocates Library in Edinburgh. In 1754 Hume was threatened with dismissal after ordering several books that the library deemed indecent.

Marcel Duchamp (1887–1968)   Conceptual artist Marcel Duchamp worked as a librarian at the Bibliothèque Sainte-Geneviève, Paris, in 1913 in order to support himself while studying maths and creating art.

Giacomo Casanova (1725–1798)   The legendary lover and carouser ended his career working as a librarian for the Count of Waldstein in Dux, Bohemia, cataloguing the Count's 40,000 volumes.

Lewis Carroll (1832–1898)   Otherwise known as Charles Lutwidge Dodgson, Lewis Carroll worked as sub-librarian at Christ Church Library in Oxford 1855–57, before becoming a lecturer in mathematics and writing *Alice's Adventures in Wonderland*.

A SHORT HISTORY OF PUBLIC LIBRARIES

The concept of a public library can be confused – some define it as a library that is open to the scholarly public but not run by a university, others as a library that is open to all, and finally some define it as a library that is supported by public taxation and open to all.

By the first definition the ancient LIBRARY OF ALEXANDRIA, which was founded in about 300 BCE, was the first public library in the world, as it was open to anyone with the correct scholarly qualifications. In Rome there were many public libraries for scholars; however, learning was made available to all by the building of rooms at bath houses where anyone could sit and read the collected scrolls – in effect a fledgling public library. In 1452, the BIBLIOTECA MALATESTIANA in Cesena, Italy, was founded: it claims to be the world's oldest public library still housed in the original building. The Biblioteca Malatestiana is certainly the oldest civic library (meaning it was owned by the commune rather than the church) in Europe.

In Britain in 1608 NORWICH PUBLIC LIBRARY opened: it was established by the city administration and was initially a reference library by subscription before books were allowed to be borrowed from 1716. CHETHAM'S LIBRARY in Manchester opened in 1653; it boasts of being the oldest surviving public library in Britain. Chetham's was established by the will of Manchester textile merchant Humphrey Chetham (1580–1653) and was intended to be a free resource for scholars of northern Britain, to rival the libraries at Oxford and Cambridge.

By the eighteenth century some libraries were beginning to lend books rather than make scholars consult the collections in reading rooms. However, the majority of libraries were not open to the general public; instead, access was only granted to scholars with the right connections.

Circulating libraries (*see page 18*) and subscription libraries flourished during the late eighteenth and nineteenth centuries but these systems both relied on an ability to pay so were not truly available to all. In America a movement for free public education for children sparked the opening of the first public library in North America when in 1833 PETERBOROUGH LIBRARY opened in New Hampshire.

The notion of a true public library, open to all and funded from taxation, was enshrined in the UK by the Public Libraries Act 1850. This led to the first true public library in Britain being opened in CAMPFIELD, Manchester, in 1852; such was its national importance that the official opening was attended by Charles Dickens and William Thackeray. This marked the beginning of a huge growth in public libraries across the UK, igniting the country's love affair with the truly public library.

THE PATRON SAINTS OF LIBRARIANS

St Lawrence of Rome was a deacon in Rome who was in charge of the church's wealth. In 258 CE the Emperor Valerian ordered that all bishops, deacons and priests should be put to death. St Lawrence quickly distributed as much of the church's riches to the poor and needy as possible, in order to prevent it falling into the emperor's hands. When St Lawrence was arrested he produced a group of paupers and cripples and declared that these people were the true treasures of the church. St Lawrence was immediately executed, supposedly on a gridiron;* hence he is invoked (somewhat insensitively) as the patron saint of cooks. St Lawrence was an archivist for the church and it is for this reason that he is also a patron saint of librarians. St Lawrence's feast day is 10 August.

St Jerome was a scholar and historian who translated the Old Testament from Greek and Hebrew into Latin, which became known as the Vulgate. Jerome helped to set up the papal library in Rome and also built up an extensive personal library of religious and pagan texts, which was unfortunately destroyed in 416 CE during the sack of Bethlehem. Due to his prolific scholarly output, Jerome is patron saint of translators,

---

* There are many depictions in art of the cruel and unusual death of St Lawrence. Legend has it that he kept his sense of humour to the end: as he was slowly being roasted on the gridiron he supposedly called out 'I'm well done. Turn me over.'

encyclopaedists and librarians. St Jerome's feast day is 30 September.

St Catherine of Alexandria had a love of learning and became a great Christian scholar. The reigning emperor was afraid of the rise of Christianity so Catherine went and debated with him: many who heard her passionate speech converted to Christianity, an action which earned them immediate execution. Catherine herself was to be put to death on a wheel;* but when she touched it, it collapsed, so instead she was beheaded. Catherine is invoked by librarians, philosophers and teachers because of her great learning, by lawyers because of her debating skills, and – rather gruesomely – by potters, millers and spinners because of her association with the wheel. St Catherine's feast day is 25 November.

LIBRARY TREASURES: WINNIE-THE-POOH

On 21 August 1921, A.A. Milne purchased a teddy bear from Harrods in London as a gift for his one-year-old son Christopher Robin. The treasured bear was at first named Edward but later renamed Winnie-the-Pooh in honour of a real bear named Winnipeg whom Christopher Robin saw at London Zoo and a swan named Pooh who featured in Milne's *When We Were*

---

* The spinning fireworks Catherine wheels are so-called in her honour.

Very Young. In 1926 A.A. Milne and illustrator E.H. Shepard brought Christopher Robin and his animal friends to life in the children's book *Winnie-the-Pooh*, immediately capturing the imagination of children everywhere. The original beloved bear and several other of Christopher Robin's (rather careworn) stuffed toys – Eeyore, Tigger, Kanga and Piglet – have, since 1987, been housed at New York Public Library, and children flock to see the inspiration behind a much-loved children's story.

A LIBRARIAN'S ALPHABET

This charming poem, composed by the mysterious M.S.G.H., appeared in the *Cheltenham Ladies' College Magazine* in 1933.

O All you young librarians, come listen unto me
If thoroughly efficient bibliographers you'd be.
But should the ensuing alphabet too long and dull be
    found,
You can fasten on the following: much Sense and little
    Sound.
And though all's not librarianship, you'd argue with
    your betters,
They're inextricably mingled, are the arts of life and
    letters.
Be ...

*A*ccurate, alert, ambitious, accessible;

*B*rief, business-like;

*C*lear, consistent, cautious, critical, capable, conscientious, calm, courteous, considerate, charitable;

*D*irect, diligent, dauntless (it's dogged as does it), disinterested;

*E*xact, enterprising, enduring, efficient;

*F*ar-seeing, fearless;

*G*allant and gay, *never* guess;

*H*onest, high-minded, humble, humorous;

*I*mpeccable, imperturbable, industrious, independent, intensely interested;

*J*udicious;

*K*nowledgeable;

*L*ucid, legible, liberal-minded, level-headed;

*M*ethodical, mindful of manners;

*N*eat, noiseless;

*O*rderly, observant, obliging;

*P*roud, prudent, precise, painstaking, persevering, punctual, patient, polite;

*Q*uick, quiet;

*R*eliable, resourceful, reasonable;

*S*ound, sensible, steady, sane;

*T*rustworthy, thorough, tireless, tactful;

*U*nderstanding;

*V*eracious, versatile, vigilant, vigorous;

*W*ise and wary, a worker;

E*X*perienced;

*Y*oung (always);

*Z*ealous.

A GLOSSARY OF LIBRARY TERMS

ABSTRACT A brief summary of the main points of a journal article

ACQUISITIONS Items purchased for library use, from books to rare maps

ALTERNATIVE FORMAT Items which are available in a non-standard format, such as braille, audio or large text

ANNOTATED BIBLIOGRAPHY A list of books with summary or critique about each work

ANNUAL A serial publication released once a year, e.g. a yearbook

ANTHOLOGY A collection of writings by different authors on the same subject or genre

ARCHIVES The place where public records or documents relating to a particular company or family are stored for posterity

BIBLIOGRAPHIC CITATION The information which identifies a book or article; for books this is usually the author, title, publisher and date of publication

BIBLIOGRAPHY A list of books, articles and sources all related to a particular subject

BINDERY Where loose pages and unbound books are sent to be repaired or bound

BLURB A short description of a book to advertise the work on a dust jacket

BOOKSTACK The area of shelving which holds a large volume of the library's stock of books: when books are ordered they are retrieved from the bookstack

BOOLEAN SEARCH The search of an online catalogue

using terms which indicate how the words being searched for relate to each other: 'and', 'not' and 'or' are the most common Boolean search terms

BOUND VOLUME A collection of periodicals bound into book form, etc.

CARD CATALOGUE Before computerized catalogues the system by which each book was recorded and catalogued

CARREL Individual study desk, often with high sides for partition

CIRCULATION DESK The desk where readers can check out items to borrow

CITATION A reference within a book or article to a source book or article

CLASSIFICATION SCHEME The method by which books are classified, e.g. by subject

CONTINUATION A serial publication issued less than three times a year and therefore not often enough to be classified as a periodical

COPYRIGHT The legal rights to the use of literary, artistic or musical works (*see page 14*)

DEWEY DECIMAL CLASSIFICATION SYSTEM A subject classification system devised by Melvil Dewey, used in many major libraries (*see page 28*)

DIGITIZATION Whereby a book or manuscript is made available in electronic form, often online

DIRECTORY List of businesses, organizations or people, giving job titles, addresses and other relevant information

EDITION An issue in print of a book, pamphlet, etc., as printed and issued at one time; a subsequent edition is a revised and republished version of the same text

ENDNOTES Notes, extra information or sources listed at the end of a literary work or periodical

EPHEMERA Items such as menus, playbills, leaflets and postcards which were not designed to last but which may have great value to social historians

FIELD Category of information, e.g. title, author, subject, by which a user may search a database or catalogue

FINE Money incurred if a borrowed item is returned late (*see page 35*)

FOOTNOTES Notes, extra information or sources listed at the bottom of the page

HOLDINGS The materials held, or owned, by the library

IMPRINT The name of a publisher, printer or distributor of a book and the date

INCUNABULA Books printed before 1501

IBSN International Standard Book Number, a unique ten- or thirteen-character number to identify each format of a book published

ISSUE A single part of a periodical as individually published

JOURNAL An academic periodical containing scholarly articles

LIBRARY CARD A card issued when a user joins the library that allows them to enter, and/or to check out items

LIBRARY OF CONGRESS CLASSIFICATION An alternative subject classification system to Dewey, originated by Library of Congress but now widespread (*see page 21*)

MAGAZINE A periodical containing popular articles

MANUSCRIPT A handwritten or typed (not printed) item

MICROFICHE A flat piece of photographic film containing images of an item

OPEN ACCESS Items which are freely available to browse on the shelves, or a publication that is freely available for anyone to read

OVERSIZE A book which is too large for standard shelves and must be stored in a special part of the library

PAMPHLET A printed item with just a few pages

PERIODICALS Items such as newspapers, magazines and journals which are published more than three times a year for an indefinite period

PUBLIC DOMAIN Materials which are not subject to copyright and so can be freely reproduced

RARE BOOK Valuable or old books, usually kept in a secure reading room

REFERENCE DESK Location in the library where the reader can seek advice in finding items

REFERENCE LIBRARIAN A specialist librarian who can help the reader to find items

RENEWAL Borrowing a book for another period of loan whilst it is still in your possession

SERIAL Items which are produced at regular intervals, e.g. journals, periodicals and magazines

SHELFMARK A unique number or letter sequence given to a book (also known as a call number or classmark) which indicates where it can be found on a shelf (*see page 101*)

SPECIAL COLLECTIONS Items outside the usual library stock which have special value (*see page 117*), e.g. ephemera, rare books or manuscripts

SUBJECT HEADING A term used to group a number of items on the same subject to aid classification and retrieval

TRADE JOURNAL A periodical title aimed at a certain specialized business sector, e.g. *Farmers' Weekly*

UNIFORM TITLE A title used for cataloguing when an item has been published under various different titles, e.g. translations

LIBRARY TREASURES: THE GOUGH MAP

The Gough Map, housed at the Bodleian Library in Oxford (MS. Gough Gen. Top. 16), is one of the earliest known maps of Britain showing it in a recognizable form. It was named in honour of the antiquarian Richard Gough (1735–1809), who bequeathed the map to the Bodleian in 1809 having acquired it from fellow antiquarian Thomas Martin. The date of the map's creation has been the subject of much research. Recent studies suggest it was created in the late fourteenth century, but the cartographer remains unknown. It is known that at least two scribes wrote the place names on the map, the earliest north of Hadrian's Wall from the fourteenth century, with revisions of the names throughout the first half of the fifteenth century south of the Wall. The map contains extraordinary levels of detail for its time, with some 600 cities, towns and settlements depicted, plus rivers and a network of red lines likely to reveal the estimated distances between key settlements. The Gough Map measures 115 cm × 56 cm and is made from parchment.

LIBRARY PHILANTHROPIST: HENRY E. HUNTINGTON

Henry Edwards Huntington (1850–1927) amassed a vast fortune over the course of a long business career in which he built up large holdings in utilities, railways and real estate in Southern California. Huntington was especially interested in collecting art and books and was also a keen gardener, ultimately creating a number of impressive botanical gardens. In 1919 Huntington established the Huntington Library in San Marino, California. The collection boasts over 7 million items and is a renowned research institution for scholars of Anglo and American history. Treasures of the collection include: a copy of the lavishly illustrated double-elephant-sized *Birds of America* by John James Audubon; the Ellesmere manuscript of Chaucer's *Canterbury Tales*; a Gutenberg Bible on vellum; and a first quarto (Q1) copy of Shakespeare's *Hamlet* (the British Library is the only other library to hold a copy of this extremely rare work).

THE UK'S BUSIEST LIBRARIES

According to statistics from the Chartered Institute of Public Finance and Accountancy (CIPFA) the following libraries were the busiest (by number of issues) in 2013/14.

LIBRARY	ISSUES
1. Norfolk and Norwich Millennium, Norfolk	1,124,406
2. The Hive, Worcester	903,859
3. Oxford Central, Oxfordshire	605,530
4. Llanelli, Carmarthenshire	601,182
5. Cardiff Central, Glamorganshire	581,779
6. Cambridge Central, Cambridgeshire	555,101
7. Chelmsford, Essex	503,233
8. Chesterfield, Derbyshire	471,792
9. West Bridgford, Nottinghamshire	457,675
10. Jubilee, Brighton & Hove	451,619

RESTRICTED TITLES IN LIBRARIES

In the nineteenth century some librarians became preoccupied with the morality or lack thereof displayed in some of their texts. Consequently a number of libraries created special shelfmarks or locations for restricted books to ensure that only readers with a proper academic purpose might access them. Below is a summary of some of the methods used to categorize restricted titles in libraries.

THE BRITISH LIBRARY'S 'PRIVATE CASE' In the British Library (or British Museum Library as it was then) it was John Winter Jones, Keeper of Printed Books from 1856, who was responsible for the creation of the 'Private Case'. Titles that were deemed subversive, heretical, libellous, contained state secrets or were considered obscene were kept out of the general catalogue, stored in separate shelving and marked with the shelfmark category 'PC' (for private case). By far the majority of books in the private case were pornographic or erotic texts. It is rumoured that by the mid-1960s the case contained over 5,000 such texts, including George Witt's collection of books on phallicism and Charles Reginald Dawes's collection of French erotica 1880–1930. What was unusual about the Private Case was that it was so secretive: none of the books at that time was recorded in any catalogue, as if the collection didn't exist. Since 1983 all books that were once in the Private Case have been listed in the catalogue and many have been returned to the main collection, although librarians may still check that a reader needs to consult some of the more scandalous titles for academic reasons.

THE VATICAN'S 'INFERNO' There has always been a rumour that the Vatican Library holds the largest collection of pornographic material in the world in a collection supposedly known as the 'inferno'.* It is thought the collection was created from the thousands of erotic works which have been confiscated by the Vatican over the years. However, no evidence for the collection has been found (and the – admittedly incredibly secretive – Vatican librarians deny its very existence).

BIBLIOTHÈQUE NATIONALE DE FRANCE, L'ENFER
L'Enfer, which translates as 'the hell', was created in 1830 to house the French national library's large collection of erotica and books considered 'contrary to good morals'. Many of the works were obtained by the library through confiscation, and fortunately the librarians had the foresight to preserve these scandalous texts. The collection was largely kept private and was only fully catalogued in 1913, recording some 855 titles. Modern pornographic magazines and erotic fiction do not get cast into L'Enfer: it is only for rare works or works of cultural significance such as a handwritten copy of the Marquis de Sade's *Les Infortunes de la Vertu* (1787) and *Story of O* by Pauline Réage (1954). In 2007 the library put on a public exhibition of some of the more fascinating (and titillating) texts in L'Enfer, finally granting the public a glimpse of this hidden collection.

---

* In fact this honour goes to the Kinsey Institute for Sex Research in Bloomington, Indiana.

NEW YORK PUBLIC LIBRARY TRIPLE-STAR COLLECTION
In the New York Public Library obscene works were
hand-marked ***, which indicated that, in order for
them to be consulted, a reader must be supervised.
This system, which began in the mid-twentieth century,
caused certain titles to be locked in caged shelves;
it meant that the items could only be consulted in a
small restricted part of the reading rooms after special
permission was granted.

BODLEIAN LIBRARY PHI COLLECTION   The restricted
collection in the Bodleian Library was created by
E.W.B. Nicholson, Bodley's Librarian 1886–1913. No
one is quite sure why it was named after the Greek
letter phi, but some suggested it was because it sounds
like 'fie!', which you might exclaim when asked to
retrieve a book from this collection, or perhaps it
stems from the first letter 'phi' of the Greek *phaula* or
phaulos, meaning worthless, wicked or base. The collection included pornography alongside works of sexual
pathology. Students needed to ask a tutor to confirm
their academic need for a book before the librarians
would let them consult any texts with a phi shelfmark.
Today many of the books have been reclassified into the
general collection, but the phi shelfmark persists, for
example to classify the pornographic magazine *Razzle*.

HARVARD'S WIDENER LIBRARY 'XR' COLLECTION
The Widener Library still holds its restricted collection behind a locked copper door in the basement of
the library, not because they still want to hide the

collection but simply because no one has the time to redistribute the collection back into main circulation. The collection was thought to have been set up in the 1950s after a sociology professor complained that many texts he needed for his class were missing or defaced (the *Playboy* centrefold was apparently always going astray): thus the restricted collection was created to protect and preserve rather than to censor. The X part of the shelfmark does not stand for X-rated but indicates that the books are unusual; the R part stands for 'restricted'. The collection was only added to for a thirty-year period and is now a closed shelfmark; however, its classification reveals something of the social attitudes of the times towards titles such as *The Passions and Lechery of Catherine the Great* (1971) and D.H. Lawrence's *Lady Chatterley's Lover* (1928).

LIBRARY TREASURES:
THE GUTENBERG BIBLE

The Gutenberg Bible was the first book in Europe to be printed using moveable type, a massive leap in technology that made books hugely more accessible. Before the advent of the printing press, creating a book was an arduous process: a scribe would take many months to copy each text by hand, making book production slow and very expensive. Printing with wooden blocks was tried, but proved more viable for pictures than for text. When Johannes Gutenberg developed the concept of moveable type and printed his first Bible in 1455 he changed the face of the book world. It is thought Gutenberg printed 180 copies of the Gutenberg Bible, some on paper and some on vellum; due to their quality and clarity Gutenberg sold every copy. Although the main body of the text was printed using moveable type, the rubrics and illuminated lettering were added by hand. Some copies of the Bible are completely unadorned. Today 49 copies of the Gutenberg Bible survive, twelve of which are on vellum: they are considered the crown of any library collection.

LIBRARY CHAIRS

For readers spending many hours in a library's reading room perhaps one of the most important aspects is the comfort (or otherwise) of their chairs. Most modern libraries take the issue of reader comfort very seriously and over the years a number of special designs have been created, often unique to a particular library, to create a seat both functional and beautiful in design. Below are several library chairs of note.

THE BRITISH LIBRARY   For the official opening of the new British Library building on Euston Road in 1998, the architect, Colin St John Wilson, tasked furniture designer Ronald Carter with creating 698 new chairs for the reading rooms. The brief was based on a painting of St Jerome (*see page 71*), the patron saint of libraries and scholars, by Antonello da Messina, which depicts Jerome seated on a curved chair, intent on his studies. Ron Carter designed a heavy oak chair with curved back, padded with green leather, which helped to create the sense of each reader's own workspace.

Bodleian Library   The Bodleian has a long history of specially designed chairs. In 1756 three dozen Windsor chairs were purchased for the library to replace the old benches: these comb-back chairs became known as Curators' Chairs. When Giles Gilbert Scott designed the New Bodleian Library in 1936 he created two new chair designs, one straight-backed and the other a bucket chair, both clad in leather, of which sixty are still in use today. During the New Bodleian's refurbishment as the Weston Library, a competition was launched to design a new Bodleian chair. In 2013 the winner was announced – an elegant three-legged oak chair designed by Edward Barber and Jay Osgerby.

New York Public Library   When architects John Merven Carrère and Thomas Hastings were engaged to design the New York Public Library building in Beaux-Arts style, they took care to design every detail from the facade to the chairs. For the Rose Main Reading Room, which opened in 1911, Carrère and Hastings designed elegant chairs made from solid red oak with arms of a curved spiral design; they are still in use today.

BIBLIOTHÈQUE NATIONALE DE FRANCE   In 1988 a new building for the French national library was designed by architect Dominique Perrault. As with many library designers, his vision included all the library furniture and fittings. Perrault selected a modern ergonomic design for the chairs, using a curved leaf of doussie (also known as afzelia) hardwood supported by metal fittings on a square wooden frame.

A CROSS-BORDER LIBRARY

Haskell Free Library and Opera House was built across the US/Canada border. Completed in 1904 by a bequest from Martha Stewart Haskell, who wanted both Canadians and Americans to have access to the library and opera, the handsome neoclassical building is deliberately located across the international border at Rock Island, Quebec and Derby Line, Vermont. Naturally the library has two different entrances, one in each country (and indeed a separate street address for each nation) and should a visitor wish to exit into the other country they must report to customs. A thick black line is painted across the floor of the reading room to indicate the international border. Although the front door is located in the USA, all the books and the circulation desk are in Canada.

UNIVERSITY LIBRARIES

University libraries are among the world's oldest, established alongside a university for the use of academics and scholars. The first university library is thought to have been the Buddhist Takshila University in what is now Pakistan, which was established in *c.* 600 BCE but is long since destroyed. Much debate surrounds the title of 'world's oldest university library', with many institutions vying for the prize. Below is a list of some of the oldest university libraries still in use today,* with the year in which they were first established.

Al-Qarawiyyin University Library, Fez	859
University of Salamanca Library, Spain	1254
Merton College Library, Oxford	1276
Bibliothèque de la Sorbonne, Paris	1289
Bodleian Library, University of Oxford†	*c.* 1320/ 1602
The Queen's College Library, Oxford	1341
Heidelberg University Library, Germany	1388
Old Library, St John's College, Cambridge	1516
Leipzig University Library, Germany	1542
Trinity College Library, Dublin	1592
Harvard University Library, USA	1638

---

* Many of the original library buildings have been replaced but the collections have persisted.

† At this time it was not known by this name: it did not become the Bodleian until Thomas Bodley refounded the university library in 1602.

THE FIRST LIBRARY CATALOGUE

Callimachus worked at the library of Alexandria under the librarian Zenodotus (*see page 92*). He was responsible for creating the first library catalogue, known as the *Pinakes*, in *c.* 245 CE. Thought to have consisted of some 120 volumes, the *Pinakes* listed all the works in the library of Alexandria by author and subject. The library at Alexandria during this period was said to contain 5,000 papyrus scrolls which were stored in bins by subject. The *Pinakes* listed all the works, categorizing them thus:

rhetoric | law | epic | tragedy | comedy
lyric poetry | history | medicine
mathematics | natural science | miscellanea

Only small fragments of the work survives today, but it seems that each scroll was categorized under one of the above subjects and then listed alphabetically by author, along with a bibliographic and critical note on the author's works. This system for producing a catalogue proved hugely influential and can be seen in many early cataloguing systems right up to the Middle Ages, including the tenth-century work by Ibn al-Nadim, the *Al-Fihrist* or *Index*, which was published in 987 and recorded all books written in Arabic at that time.

LIBRARY TREASURES:
THE BOOK OF KELLS

Ireland's foremost medieval treasure the Book of Kells is a beautiful illuminated copy of the four Gospels based upon the Latin Vulgate. It is thought to have been created by Columban* monks in *c.* 800, possibly on the Scottish Island of Iona, and, after Viking raids dispersed the monastic community, to have been taken to Ireland. The quality of the illustration and illumination in the Book of Kells is outstanding: it is a remarkable example of Western calligraphy and Insular art. The manuscript is made up of 340 folios on parchment, which since 1953 have been bound together into four volumes. The book was so-called because it was housed at the Abbey of Kells in County Meath during the medieval period. It was gifted to Trinity College Library, Dublin in 1661, where it remains to this day. The library displays two volumes of the Book of Kells at any one time, with one open at pages of text, the other showing one of the ornate illustrations.

---

* St Columbanus (543–615) was an Irish missionary who founded many monasteries in the Frankish and Lombard kingdoms and created a Celtic tradition of monastic rules.

THE WORLD'S FIRST
RECORDED LIBRARIAN

Zenodotus of Ephesus was superintendent of the library at Alexandria (which was established *c.* 300 BCE) during the reigns of the first two Ptolemies and may be considered the world's first recorded librarian. Alongside his work in the library, Zenodotus was a grammarian and scholar and produced the first critical edition of Homer. During his tenure as librarian at Alexandria, Zenodotus introduced a system to classify the books by subject matter, by assigning them to different rooms in the library and then arranging them alphabetically by the first letter of the author's name. It is thought this was the first use of alphabetization in a library.

SEED LIBRARIES

A seed library is a way for a community to share and preserve seeds. Some seed libraries are housed alongside a more traditional book collection and are a free resource (or may have a nominal membership fee) to encourage the local community to take away seeds to grow food and then return any spare seeds they produce. Seed libraries are often especially focused on preserving heritage crops which may not be available from commercial seed nurseries, or on collecting seed varieties which are native to the region. There has been some controversy over seed libraries in America, where since 2012 state department of agriculture officials have invoked commercial regulations on some seed libraries, causing them to be shut down. Fortunately a number of states have now passed laws which protect seed libraries and the network is once again growing.

'LET ME LIBRARIAN THAT FOR YOU'

Since 2015 New York Public Library has been sharing on social media (on its Instagram feed and on Twitter via the hashtag #letmelibrarianthatforyou) some of its quirkiest enquiries from its archive. The requests, which were recorded and preserved on question cards, reveal the huge breadth of knowledge the public expected their sagacious librarians to display in an era before Google. Below are some of the most charming questions posed to New York librarians.

- 'What is the significance of the hip movement in the Hawaiian dance?' (July 1944)
- 'Please give me the name of a book that dramatizes bedbugs?' (September 1944)
- 'Wanted: a list of historical characters who were in the right place at the right time.' (September 1946)
- 'Is this the place where I ask questions I can't get answers to?' (September 1947)
- 'What kind of apple did Eve eat?' (September 1956)

- 'When was the Battle of Armageddon fought, and who won – what was the outcome?' (October 1960)
- 'Is there a law in NYC whereby a child can become unrelated to its parent if they don't like each other?' (February 1961)
- 'Is there a book on how to build with popsicle sticks?' (March 1967)
- 'Why do 18th-century English paintings have so many squirrels in them, and how did they tame them so that they wouldn't bite the painter?' (October 1976)
- 'What do you feed a salamander?' (November 1983)
- 'Can you tell me who painted the picture of Whistler's mother?' (undated)

LEGAL DEPOSIT AROUND THE WORLD

The rules regarding legal deposit differ around the world, but the most common regulation is that at least one copy of every book published must be sent to the national library in order to preserve the nation's published heritage. These days most legal deposit applies not just to books but also to maps, musical scores, periodicals and in some cases digital and audiovisual output. The number of copies of books required to be deposited with the national library (and in some cases at other specified libraries around the country in question) in countries around the world are as follows:

COUNTRY	NATIONAL LIBRARY	COPIES
Australia	National Library of Australia, Canberra	1
Canada	Library and Archives Canada, Ottawa	2
China	National Library of China, Beijing	3
France	National Library of France, Paris	1
Germany	German National Library, Leipzig and Frankfurt am Main	2
India	National Library of India, Kolkata	1
Malaysia	National Library of Malaysia, Kuala Lumpar	5
Portugal	National Library of Portugal, Lisbon	11
Russia	Russian State Library, Moscow	1
South Africa	National Library of South Africa, Cape Town	5
United Kingdom	The British Library, London*	1
USA	Library of Congress, Washington DC	2

---

* For more on legal deposit in the United Kingdom, see page 14.

LIBRARY PHILANTHROPIST:
JOHN RYLANDS

John Rylands (1801–1888) was Manchester's first multimillionaire, making his fortune from textile manufacturing. A shrewd businessman who built his firm from a small textile factory into the largest textile manufacturer and merchant in the UK, at its peak employing over 15,000 people in seventeen mills and factories, Rylands had a strong social conscience and throughout his lifetime financed many orphanages and homes for the elderly in Manchester. A keen book collector, he donated his private library as the basis of the John Rylands Library in Manchester, which was opened in 1900 by his wife Enriqueta in his memory.

The library now forms part of Manchester University Library and is home to extensive special collections, including some 3,000 incunabula, a number of books printed by William Caxton, the Rylands Papyri (which include the St John's Fragment, perhaps the earliest New Testament text) and a first edition of *Ulysses* by James Joyce.

CARD CATALOGUES

Library catalogues have been in use since the earliest libraries (*see page 90*) but it was not until the end of the eighteenth century that card catalogues were first developed. Early library catalogues were in the form of books: as new titles were added to the collection they would have to be recorded in the margins until a revised catalogue was produced. Thus the system of card catalogues was especially useful in a growing collection, because each book or item is recorded on one card and then filed in a card catalogue drawer alphabetically: this means that new entries can easily be added and old entries simply amended by replacing the index card.

The system was created in France, where in the aftermath of the Revolution books from monasteries and the collections of the nobility were confiscated in order to create a system of public libraries: to do this an inventory of all books was required. The French Cataloguing Code of 1791 gave instructions on how the books should be listed, with the bibliographic detail of each title being recorded on the blank reverse of playing cards – thus the catalogue card was born. Each card would be given a keyword, usually the author's surname or the subject of the book, which would be underlined. The cards were then sorted alphabetically by keyword and sewn together through the lower left-hand corner.

By the mid-nineteenth century the card catalogue method had been introduced in American libraries. Charles Folsom, the librarian at the Boston Athenaeum, wrote of his card catalogue system in 1853:

> [It] consisted of a series of cards, about nine inches long and two wide, which were laid in a pile and a hole bored through each end of the whole, and strings passed through them. These strings were of such a length as to allow the whole of the cards to be slid back or forward, as the writer or compositor should find necessary, yet still preserving them in their proper order, without confusion or danger of loss. The whole were fitted into a box of the requisite size, from which they could be drawn singly without deranging the consecutiveness of each.

In 1862, Harvard Library created a card catalogue for public use, the cards being 5 × 12.25 cm (known as Harvard College size) and placed between wooden blocks to keep them upright. In the first year some 35,762 cards were created. From 1877 the American Library Association standardized the size of catalogue cards, using the Harvard College size and the 'postal' size, which was 7.5 × 12.25 cm; the second of these became standard across American libraries. Catalogue cards were at first written by hand, so legible handwriting was essential for librarians (*see page 44*).

Wooden cabinets with many drawers were created to hold the library card catalogue, allowing the cards to be easily consulted and added to. Melvil Dewey, who developed the Dewey subject classification system (*see page 28*), set up the Library Bureau in 1881 to provide supplies to libraries; by 1886 they advertised a number of card catalogue cabinets.

The system of card catalogues became the most common cataloguing system across America and Europe, and card catalogue cabinets became a common sight. Although the system was user-friendly and grew with the collection, it also had a number of drawbacks, such as the lack of uniform style in the format of the catalogue: this meant that the cards were constantly having to be amended to keep up with the current system. But the main disadvantage was the amount of space they took up – a library with a large collection might have to devote a whole room to cabinets filled with the card catalogue, meaning less space for study and book storage.

As computerized catalogues were developed from the 1970s, the old-fashioned method of card catalogue was slowly abandoned. In 2015 the Online Computer Library Center (OCLC), the company which printed out catalogue cards for American libraries, officially ceased production of catalogue cards, formally ending this now outmoded cataloguing system.

JOHN DEE'S LOST LIBRARY

John Dee (1527–1609) was a fascinating Tudor poly-math who inhabited many roles – magician, mathematician, astronomer, alchemist and spy. Dee's library at his home in Mortlake was once one of the finest in Europe – said to include some 3,000 books and 1,000 manuscripts. Unfortunately when Dee travelled to Europe in the 1580s his unscrupulous brother-in-law, Nicholas Fromond, who had been left in charge of the library, sold most of the books. On his return, Dee was horrified by the destruction of his marvellous collection and tried to trace as many of the texts as possible, but the majority were lost. However, at least 100 books stolen from Dee's personal collection were later acquired by Henry Pierrepont, 1st Marquis of Dorchester and from his collection were bequeathed to the Royal College of Physicians Library in 1680, which holds them to this day. Some of the most fascinating aspects of the books from Dee's collection are the notes and drawings he made in the margins, revealing something of his thoughts and personality. The surviving works in Dee's library include:

- *Mathemalogium prime partis* by Andreas Alexander (1504) – on mathematics and Aristotle
- *Opera* by Arnaldus de Villanova (1527) – on alchemy
- *De thermis* by Andrea Bacci (1571) – on baths and bathing

- *Libelli quinque* by Girolamo Cardano (1547) – on astrology
- *Belli Troiani scriptores praecipui* (1573) – a compilation on the Trojan War
- *Canones super novum instrumentum luminarium* by Sebastian Münster (1534) – on astronomical instruments[*]

SHELFMARKS AND CLASSMARKS

A shelfmark or classmark is a group of numbers and/or letters which relate to where in a library a book can be found. Shelfmarks and classmarks are often grouped by subject so that all items under a specific subject heading will be kept together in one area, making it easier to browse. There is no single standardized way of organizing a shelfmark or classmark and many libraries have created their own systems, some of which, due to the way they have developed over a long history, are fairly archaic. The two most widely used are the Library of Congress Subject Classification (*see page 21*) and the Dewey Decimal Classification system (*see page 28*), in which items are classified using a combination of letters to indicate the subject, and numbers to reveal the shelf location. The shelfmark or classmark is usually displayed on the spine of the book to allow it to be consulted easily.

---

[*] Dee's copy contains many annotations, including some meteorological and astrological observations from Louvain which he recorded in August and December 1548.

LIBRARIES ON FILM

The following famous libraries have been used as film sets:

THE LIBRARY OF CONGRESS, WASHINGTON DC
All the President's Men (1976), *National Treasure* (2004)

BODLEIAN LIBRARY, OXFORD
The Madness of King George (1994), *Tinker, Tailor, Soldier, Spy* (2011), *X-Men: First Class* (2011), the *Harry Potter* movies, as Hogwarts Library.

NEW YORK PUBLIC LIBRARY
Breakfast at Tiffany's (1961), *Ghostbusters* (1984), *The Thomas Crown Affair* (1999), *Spider-Man* (2002), *The Day After Tomorrow* (2004), *Sex and the City: The Movie* (2008), *Oblivion* (2013)

HUNTINGTON LIBRARY, CALIFORNIA
Indecent Proposal (1993), *The Nutty Professor* (1996), *Serenity* (2005), *Memoirs of a Geisha* (2005), *Iron Man 2* (2010)

STRAHOV MONASTERY LIBRARY, PRAGUE
From Hell (2001), *Dungeons and Dragons* (2000), *The League of Extraordinary Gentlemen* (2003), *Casino Royale* (2006)

SOME UK PUBLIC LIBRARY FACTS

A 2016 investigation by the BBC revealed that government cuts to public services in the UK have had a significant effect on public libraries. Many have been forced to close – between 2010 and 2016 some 343 libraries were closed and 111 were at risk of closure. Some libraries have cut staff, using volunteers in their place, resulting in a 25 per cent drop in paid library staff. The following facts and statistics from the Chartered Institute of Public Finance and Accountancy (CIPFA) give a snapshot of the UK's public libraries.

LARGEST	
UK	Library of Birmingham
Europe	Library of Birmingham
FIRST	Chetham's Library, Manchester (open continuously since 1653)
SMALLEST	Many traditional red telephone boxes repurposed as informal public libraries
MOST POPULAR	
visits	Central Manchester (1,332,999 visits 2014/15)
loans	Norfolk and Norwich Millennium Library (1,012,877 loans 2014/15)
PUBLIC LIBRARIES	
UK 2002/03	4,620
UK 2014/15	3,917

MODERN BOOK STORAGE

Today large modern libraries are required to store a huge amount of material, especially those libraries with responsibility for legal deposit (*see page 14*). In recent years a number of modern book storage warehouses have opened up in order to provide a large space to safely store low-usage items, such as books, journals and magazines. The British Library's warehouse in Boston Spa, Yorkshire, opened in 2009 and has space for over 7 million items. The items are kept in special bar-coded boxes, allowing robots to find and retrieve items requested by readers. The warehouse is kept at low oxygen density to help protect the books from damage – normal air has 20 per cent oxygen but Boston Spa is kept at between 15.8 and 16.2 per cent. The air conditioning keeps the temperature constant and ensures optimum relative humidity at around 52 per cent. Like the British Library, the Bodleian Library in Oxford uses a state-of-the-art warehouse to store its low-usage items. The Book Storage Facility (BSF) opened in 2010 just outside Swindon can hold 8.4 million items on 153 miles of shelving. The books are stored on 11-metre-tall bookcases, with different sized shelves to accommodate a variety of book sizes, and are kept in 745,000 bar-coded trays to make retrieval more simple. The BSF also contains over 600 map cabinets, which hold 1.2 million maps and items in a large format.

SOME VERY OVERDUE LIBRARY BOOKS

Most people have experienced the shame of having to pay a library fine after forgetting to return a book on time, but some people have taken it to extremes. The following are some of the most overdue library books ever recorded:

In 1789 President George Washington borrowed a law treatise titled *The Law of Nations* from the New York Society Library; 221 years later, in 2010, the staff at his former Mount Vernon home finally got round to returning the book on his behalf. Grateful for the book's return, the library decided to waive the $300,000 fine.

In 2012 the librarians of Chicago Public Library decided to hold an amnesty on all late fines and were delighted to have some 100,000 books, DVDs and audiobooks returned to them. The cache included a rare edition of *The Picture of Dorian Gray* by Oscar Wilde, which had been taken out in 1934.

An anonymous reader posted a very overdue book, *The Real Book about Snakes,* back to Champaign County Library in Ohio in 2013 with the following note: 'Sorry I've kept this book so long, but I'm a really slow reader! I've enclosed my fine of $299.30 (41 years, 2 cents a day). Once again, my apologies.'

A university professor noticed a book in his collection which he had taken out from Queen's University

Library in Belfast when he was a student there in 1966; realizing his error, he returned *The Poems of Arthur Hugh Clough* with his sincere apologies. Happy to have the book back, the library overlooked the £8,577.50 fine.

In 2011 Camden School of Arts lending library in Australia had a first edition of Charles Darwin's *Insectivorous Plants* returned to them. The book had been checked out in 1889 and had lain among the book collection of a retired veterinarian before the library stamp was noticed and the book returned, some 122 years late.

THE AMERICAN LIBRARY IN PARIS

In an unprepossessing building in the 7th arrondissement of Paris is housed an American library holding 120,000 books – the largest English-language lending library in continental Europe. The not-for-profit library was established in 1920 after World War I from the thousands of books which had been sent to troops in the trenches by the American War Service. After the war ended the books were collected into a library whose motto reflects its origins and ethos: *Atrum post bellum, ex libris lux* (After the darkness, the light of books). During World War II the library was able to stay open and largely uncensored thanks to the fact that its director's son was married to the daughter of Vichy prime minister Pierre Laval. The library secretly used its position to lend books to Jews who had been banned from other libraries. Many notable expat writers have used the library, including Archibald MacLeish, Edith Wharton, Ernest Hemingway and Gertrude Stein, and it continues to be a haven for English-speaking writers and expats alike.

PRISON LIBRARIES

The first prison libraries contained mainly religious texts, in an effort to reform the bad characters imprisoned within. The first prison in America to contain books was in Nantucket, Massachusetts, built in 1676; its collection was almost entirely composed of copies of the Bible. It was not until 1820 that the first official prison library in America was built at Kentucky State Prison, and again its focus was on religious texts. By the 1940s and 1950s attitudes in America had changed and prison libraries became more important, moving away from just stocking religious texts to become more like ordinary lending libraries. However, American prison libraries to this day apply a great deal of censorship to their collections: books covering homosexuality, gang-related materials and references to the Civil Rights Movement are banned in some American prison libraries because they are deemed too inflammatory.

As in America, UK prisons initially held mainly religious libraries with improving texts, but since 1999 all prisons in England and Wales have legally been required to have a library and to employ a qualified librarian. Prisoners must have access to books and be allowed to borrow books from the library – prisoners are allowed up to twelve books in their cells at any one time (this includes books from their own collection as well as library books). Ministry of Justice guidelines stipulate that the stock of a prison library should be ten times greater than the prison population itself. Reading and education levels among prisoners are much lower than among the general population, and thus it is seen as a vital part of rehabilitation to offer prisoners access to books.

UNESCO'S WORLD DIGITAL LIBRARY

In 2005 James H. Billington, Librarian of Congress, proposed to UNESCO the creation of an online digital library showcasing the cultural content from many of the libraries of the world. The project was given the go-ahead and recruited partner organizations such as the National Library and Archives of Egypt and the National Library of Russia to begin developing a platform. The World Digital Library was formally launched in 2009 with items from twenty-six institutions across nineteen countries. Today the World Digital Library has digitized and made available for free thousands of cultural treasures and historical documents, including manuscripts, maps, journals, photographs and films.

LIBRARY TREASURES:
THE DECLARATION OF INDEPENDENCE

The Library of Congress in Washington DC holds a draft, handwritten by Thomas Jefferson, of the Declaration of Independence (manuscript division 49). Jefferson was selected by the representatives of the thirteen colonies which were declaring independence from Great Britain, as he was seen as the best writer. The library also holds a fragment of the very first draft that Jefferson composed, in mid-June 1776, which was heavily edited. The full rough draft was copied and expanded from this fragment and contains edits by John Adams and Benjamin Franklin. It is from this draft that scholars can see how the wording changed between the initial idea and the actual Declaration, which was signed on 4 July 1776.

MOST POPULAR LIBRARY LOANS BY GENRE

Libraries are still hugely popular across the UK, with a January 2014 YouGov survey revealing that 51 per cent of the UK population has a valid library card and 47 per cent had used a public library within the last twelve months. The statistics below reveal the breakdown of the UK's borrowing habits by genre, indicating that fiction continues to dominate the nation's reading habits.*

SUBJECT CATEGORY	LOANS (%)
Law	0.1
Medicine	0.1
Earth Sciences, Geography, Environment, Planning	0.1
Technology, Engineering, Agriculture	0.1
Reference, Information and Interdisciplinary Subjects	0.1
English Language Teaching (ELT)	0.3
Language	0.4
Literature and Literary Studies	0.4
Mathematics and Science	0.4
Economics, Finance, Business, Management	0.5
Computing and Information Technology	0.7
Society and Social Sciences	0.9

---

* For the period 2014/15, sourced from PLR UK.

RMS *TITANIC* LIBRARY

The RMS *Titanic* had two libraries aboard, one in the first-class lounge, the other in the second-class lounge. Both libraries were overseen by Thomas Kelland, the library steward, who unfortunately perished when the *Titanic* sank. Lawrence Beesley, a young science teacher who survived the disaster, described the library in his book *The Loss of the SS Titanic*, which was published in 1912, just three months after the sinking:

> The library was crowded that afternoon, owing to the cold on deck: but through the windows we could see the clear sky with the brilliant sunlight that seemed to augur a fine night and a clear to-morrow, and the prospect of landing in two days, with calm weather all the way to New York, was a matter of general satisfaction among us all. I can look back and see every detail of the library that

afternoon – the beautifully furnished room, with lounges, armchairs, and small writing or card-tables scattered about, writing-bureaus around the walls of the room, and the library in glass-cased shelves flanking one side – the whole finished in mahogany relieved with white fluted wooden columns that supported the deck above.

The sinking of the *Titanic* produced other ripples for the library world. Book collector and Harvard graduate Harry Elkins Widener perished in the disaster and as a result his mother, Eleanor Elkins Widener, endowed a library in his honour at Harvard.* The Harry Elkins Widener Memorial Library was established in 1915 and holds Widener's personal book collection of 3,300 rare works at its heart.

LIBRARY RULES

Most people, when they picture a library, imagine a place of silence, perhaps with a stern librarian peering over their half-moon glasses while emitting a fierce 'Shhhhh!' Many libraries hold similar rules: below is a selection from around the world.

---

* A legend persists that due to her son's fate, Mrs Widener made it a condition of her donation that all students must learn to swim. A second myth tells that she bequeathed an extra pot of money to ensure that all students could daily have ice cream for pudding as it was her son's favourite dessert. Unfortunately there is no evidence that either of these charming requests is true.

Cambridge University Library

- Silence shall be maintained as far as possible in the Library.
- Overcoats, raincoats, and other kinds of outdoor clothing, umbrellas, bags, cases, photocopying devices, and similar personal belongings shall normally be deposited in the locker-room adjacent to the entrance hall during each visit to the Library.
- Bottles of ink, correction fluid, and other potentially damaging substances shall not be taken into the Library.

Bodleian Library, Oxford

- You may not bring animals into a library, with the exception of assistance dogs
- You must follow all other reasonable requests of library staff.
- Do not engage in the harassment of any other reader, member of library staff or visitor.

The British Library, London

- Consider other Readers and behave in a way that does not disturb them and respects their privacy. If it is necessary to talk, please do so quietly.
- When using the internet, please ensure that others are not exposed to extreme or unpleasant visual material that may either offend or distress.
- Mobile phones must either be turned off or on silent mode. Calls must not be made or received and texting kept to a minimum.
- Writing in or marking collection material is not permitted in any form.

- Items that could harm the collections are not allowed in the Reading Rooms. These include, but are not limited to: pens, 'Post-It' notes, food, drink, sweets (including cough sweets), chewing gum, glue, bottles of ink, correction fluid, cleaning liquids, scissors, knives (including craft knives and razor blades), highlighter pens, scanner pens, portable scanners, adhesive tape and umbrellas.

Vatican Library

- Readers admitted to the Library are required to observe strict silence not only in the reading rooms, but within the entire premises, conversing only in the courtyard or in the Library bar.
- It is forbidden to disturb the study and work of other readers, e.g. by talking out loud or by using any kind of noisy equipment.
- Readers must wear attire appropriate to the dignity of an ancient institution of culture and study.
- Mobile phones must be turned off at the entrance. It is absolutely forbidden to use any electronic means of communication within the Library.
- All readers are required to conduct themselves in a manner befitting the decorum of the Library.
- Behaviour by individuals or groups which is inappropriate to the dignity of the institution is forbidden.

New York Public Library

The following are NOT allowed at The New York Public Library:

- Engaging in conduct that disrupts or interferes with normal operation of the Library, or that disturbs staff or other Library visitors. Such conduct includes:
- Harassing or threatening behavior.
- Using obscene or abusive language or gestures.
- Making unreasonable noise, including loud talking on a cell phone or otherwise.
- Engaging in sexual conduct or lewd behavior.
- Having a knife, gun, or any other weapon.
- Smoking.
- Eating or drinking except in designated areas.
- Using alcohol or illegal drugs.
- Sleeping in the Library or at the Library's entrance.
- Making unreasonable use of the rest rooms, including laundering clothes and bathing.
- Soliciting, petitioning, or canvassing.
- Selling any goods or services.
- Using a bicycle, skates, skateboard, scooter, or anything like them.

NATIONAL LIBRARY OF CHINA

- Any other activities irrelevant to services provided by the National Library of China are prohibited in the Library.
- Do not bring food or drinks to the Library.
- Smoking is prohibited within the Library. Inflammable, explosive or toxic and dangerous items are not allowed in the Library.
- Readers should be aware of their appearance, be dressed decently and be polite and civilized in the Library.

LIBRARY TREASURES: BAY PSALM BOOK

The Bay Psalm Book was the first book to be printed in North America, in 1640; eleven copies are known to have survived, and of these only five are complete, making it an exceedingly valuable book.* The book is a series of metred psalms intended to be sung by the settlers of the new colony of Massachusetts Bay. The equipment for the printing press had been shipped over from England by Reverend Jose Glover and his wife Elizabeth; unfortunately Jose died aboard ship and it was left to Elizabeth and Stephen Daye, Glover's apprentice, to set up the very first printing press in America. It is estimated that 1,700 copies of the book were printed by Stephen Daye. As it was an early endeavour for the former locksmith, the book contains many rather charming typographical and printing errors. All eleven surviving first-edition copies are currently housed in institutions around the world:

Library of Congress | Yale University Library
Harvard University Library | Bodleian Library†
Brown University Library | Huntington Library
American Antiquarian Society | Duke University
New York Public Library | Boston Public Library
Rosenbach Museum & Library

---

* A copy sold at auction in 2013 for $14.2 million, making it the most expensive printed book ever sold. The buyer, David M. Rubenstein, loaned it to Duke University.

† The Bodleian's copy comes from the collection of Bishop Thomas Tanner; it is the only copy of the Bay Psalm Book outside North America.

SOME CURIOUS SPECIAL COLLECTIONS OF NOTE

A special collection is usually a collection of books, manuscripts or archives which has been created and kept by an individual before being donated to or bought by a library. Due to the often unique contents of these collections they are kept intact as a body of books rather than being dispersed among the general collection.

Libraries around the world hold some fascinating and surprising special collections, often created by captivating individuals. Below are some curious special collections of note:

THE JOHN JOHNSON COLLECTION OF PRINTED EPHEMERA   Held at the Bodleian Library in Oxford, the John Johnson Collection is one of the world's largest collections of printed ephemera. Mostly covering the eighteenth to early twentieth centuries, the collection comprises everyday printed items such as leaflets, adverts, pamphlets, greeting cards, menus and postcards, lending a fascinating glimpse into Britain's social history.

THE JOHN G. WHITE CHESS AND CHEQUERS COLLECTION AT CLEVELAND PUBLIC LIBRARY Cleveland resident John Griswold White (1845–1928) was the president of Cleveland Public Library Board of Trustees; throughout his tenure he helped to grow the library's special collection, including the hugely important chess and chequers collection. One of the largest in the world, it contains over 30,000 books on chess and chequers plus chess pieces, tournament records and letters from luminaries of the chess world such as Bobby Fischer.

The Women's Library at the London School of Economics   The Women's Library documents the huge social change in women's lives since the mid-nineteenth century through books, pamphlets, periodicals, archives, and museum items relating to the suffrage movement.

Tobacciana collection at New York Public Library   George Arents, one of the founders of the American Tobacco Company, donated his collection of books, ephemera and accessories relating to the history and use of tobacco to New York Public Library in 1944. It is considered the world's largest collection of tobacciana. Highlights include: 125,000 cigarette cards; a copy of Martin Waldseemüller's *Cosmographiae Introductio*, published in 1507, with the first known description of tobacco use; and a pewter snuff box once owned by Charles Dickens.

The Sudan Archive at Durham University Library   Donated in 1957, the Sudan Archive is a collection of over 800 boxes of papers, 50,000 photographs, 1,000 maps and many museum objects all relating to the Anglo-Egyptian Condominium (1899–1956) when England effectively ruled over Sudan.

LUDVIG F.A. WIMMER'S COLLECTION OF RUNOLOGY AT THE ROYAL LIBRARY OF DENMARK Donated to the library in 1915, the collection includes the drawings and cardboard impressions used for the first scholarly edition of Danish runic inscriptions, which was published between 1895 and 1908. It also includes some 600 volumes on runes and runic inscriptions.

MASS OBSERVATION ARCHIVE AT THE UNIVERSITY OF SUSSEX The Mass Observation project, begun in 1937, sought to gather the opinions of ordinary British people on everything from the impact of rationing during the war to reactions to the death of Diana, Princess of Wales. The archive includes research materials, personal letters, photographs and diaries, and provides a fascinating look at British life.

THE CIRCUS COLLECTION AT THE BIBLIOTHÈQUE NATIONALE DE FRANCE The Performing Arts Department at the Bibliothèque nationale in Paris brings together a number of special collections on the art of the circus. The collections include photographs, clown costumes, costume designs and circus posters.

THE NURSE ROMANCE NOVEL COLLECTION A collection of around 425 romance books from 1950 to the 1970s with nurses as central characters is held at the University of Wisconsin–Milwaukee Library. Gathered together by the artist Professor Leslie Bellavance for her research on the representation of nurses in popular culture, the unique collection was donated in 2005.

CHILDREN'S LIBRARIES

Separate provision for children in libraries was slow to come about, due perhaps in part to the Victorian idea that 'children should be seen but not heard'. However, following the introduction of state education in Britain in 1870, when children's literacy rates began to burgeon, there became a real need for children's books in libraries. Keeping noisy children away from quiet adult reading rooms was another consideration in the development of children's spaces in libraries.

It is thought the first separate building for children was built at Nottingham Public Library in 1882, but it was in America where the concept of a dedicated children's library really took root. In 1890 Brookline Public Library in Massachusetts established a children's room, and in 1895 Boston Public Library opened its children's room with 3,000 books in easy reach of young readers. British librarian Stanley Jast, who visited America in 1903, wrote of his experiences of the children's libraries there:

> The children's rooms which you get in all
> the new buildings are exceedingly fine,
> beautiful apartments, the woodwork often
> beautifully carved, and so on. At the recently
> opened Pacific Branch at Brooklyn there is
> a magnificent fireplace and an ingle nook in
> which the children can sit close to the fire

on winter evenings and read their books ...
There are good pictures on the walls, and the
higher shelves are covered with wooden flaps,
[in turn] covered with green baize, on which
pictures are fastened. The whole appearance
of the room is bright and gay, the appeal being
constantly to the eye as well as the mind of the
child.*

However, many of these early children's libraries were
nothing like the bright, playful spaces we are used to
seeing in libraries today. Instead they were based upon
the schoolroom, with lines of desks and plain white-
washed walls. It was not until the 1920s and 1930s
that children's rooms in libraries began to become
more child-friendly spaces, with areas for storytelling
sessions and bright displays. By 1937 an Association of
Children's Librarians had been established in the UK
(it merged with the Libraries Association in 1947),
indicating that a dedicated children's library service
had become essential to public libraries across Britain
and beyond.

---

* 'Some Impressions of American Libraries', *Library Association Record*
7 (1905).

WHITE GLOVES

A myth has persisted that when handling rare books or manuscripts a pair of white gloves should be worn. So far has this image lodged in the national consciousness that when experts are pictured on television not wearing gloves the public have been known to phone in to complain. Such was the frequency with which complaints were being received about the lack of white gloves that the British Library produced some official guidelines in 2011. The guidelines set out that white gloves (or indeed gloves of any colour) reduce manual dexterity and can cause damage to delicate materials; in fact clean, dry, bare hands are by far the most effective and safe way of handling old texts.

LIBRARY TREASURES:
THE QUEDLINBURG *ITALA* FRAGMENT

The Quedlinburg *Itala* fragment is the oldest surviving illustrated biblical manuscript in the world. The fragments represent six folios, which would have originally been from a large illuminated book containing at least part of the Bible, thought to have been created in Rome *c.* 420. The leaves were found in parts in 1865, 1866 and 1867 in Quedlinburg, Germany, where they had been reused in the bindings of seventeenth-century books. The delicate surviving pages contain Latin text from the Old Testament Book of I Samuel and fourteen miniature illustrations in the style of late antiquity. Beneath the fading pictures can be seen instructions to the artist about which scenes to draw, giving valuable insight into methods of book production during this period. Since 1875 the fragments have been part of the Berlin State Library collection (Staatsbibliothek Preussischer Kulturbesitz, Cod. theol. lat. fol. 485).

THE FOUNDATION COLLECTIONS OF THE BRITISH LIBRARY

When the British Museum was founded in 1753 its manuscript collection, which would later form the basis of the British Library, consisted of three exceptional collections, now known as the foundation collections. The foundation collections are as follows:

THE COTTON COLLECTION
Sir Robert Cotton (1571–1631) over the course of his lifetime created an amazing library of British literature, history and religious content. Cotton's library contained fourteen bookcases, each with the bust of a different Roman emperor above. Each shelf was given a letter and every volume a Roman numeral. This meant that all his books had very clear shelfmarks, which persist to this day. For example, the celebrated Lindisfarne Gospels, the jewel of his collection, has the

shelfmark Cotton Nero D IV. Cotton's collection was bequeathed to the nation in 1702 by his grandson Sir John Cotton. In 1731, during a period of temporary storage at Ashburnham House, the collection suffered a serious fire which destroyed a few manuscripts and damaged many more.

THE HARLEIAN COLLECTION

The 1st Earl of Oxford, Robert Harley (1661–1724), together with his son, the 2nd Earl of Oxford, Edward Harley (1689–1741) created an extraordinary collection of manuscripts. Mostly German, French and Italian, the manuscripts date from the Early Middle Ages to the Renaissance and include many important religious works such as the early-ninth-century Book of Nunnaminster (Harl. 2965) and two volumes of a thirteenth-century *Bible moralisée* (Harl. 1526 and 1527).

THE SLOANE COLLECTION

Physician, collector and scientist Sir Hans Sloane (1660–1753) amassed a vast collection of plant specimens, antiquities, curios, books and manuscripts. They were purchased for the nation in 1753. Sloane's objects became the basis for the British Museum's collection and his manuscripts a basis for the British Library. Sloane's manuscript collection is especially rich in texts on natural history, science and medicine, and includes early treatises on surgery and some wonderful medieval bestiaries.

DEVELOPMENT OF LIBRARIES: TIMELINE

c. 627 BCE — The Library of Ashurbanipal established near Ninevah, Assyria (now Iraq)

c. 600 BCE — The first university library established, the Buddhist Takshila in Pakistan

c. 300 BCE — The Ancient Library of Alexandria established

c. 245 BCE — The *Pinakes* (*see page 90*), the world's first known library catalogue, produced for the Library of Alexandria

197–59 BCE — Pergamon Library in Turkey established by Eumenes II

28 BCE — The Library of Apollo (Palatine Library) in Rome opened

132 CE — The Library of Hadrian in Athens created

c. 150–450 — The codex, the ancestor of the modern book, developed

c. 357 — The Imperial Library at Constantinople established by Constantius II

c. 563 — St Columba established a monastery, library and scriptorium on the Scottish island of Iona; it is thought to be here that the Book of Kells (*see page 91*) was written *c.* 800

1204 — Crusaders destroyed the Imperial Library at Constantinople

1227	The House of Wisdom, with 80,000 volumes, established in Baghdad, Iraq
1258	Mongol invaders destroyed the House of Wisdom, and the Tigris River reportedly ran 'black with ink'
1289	University of Paris, Sorbonne Library opened
1345	The earliest book on librarianship, *Philobiblon* by bishop Richard de Bury (1287–1345), was written
1370–1420	Gloucester Cathedral built twenty stone carrels, with windows above to provide light, for monks to read and write
1371	Merton College Library in Oxford opened; still in continuous daily use
1452	Biblioteca Malatestiana in Cesena, Italy, opened: the world's oldest public library
1455	The first book printed with moveable type, the Gutenberg Bible (*see page 85*), printed in Germany
1476	William Caxton introduced the first printing press to Britain
1481	A catalogue produced by the Vatican Library revealed it contained 3,500 volumes by this time
1536–41	Henry VIII dissolved hundreds of English monasteries, leading to the break-up of many great libraries

1602	The Bodleian Library at Oxford was opened by Sir Thomas Bodley, refounding the old university library
1610	Thomas Bodley reached an agreement with the Stationers' Company that a copy of every book published in England would be deposited at his library in Oxford, and the concept of legal deposit was born (*see page 14*)
1612	The Vatican Secret Archive established
1638	John Harvard bequeathed over 400 books to establish the Harvard University Library
1653	Chetham's Library in Manchester was endowed as a free public reference library
1692	The French royal library in Paris (now the Bibliothèque nationale de France) opened to the public, the first free national library to do so
1710	The Statute of Anne, the first copyright law in the world, was passed, giving a term of fourteen years' copyright
1731	Benjamin Franklin opened the first Philadelphia Library Company, a subscription-based library
1747	The Redwood Library and Athenaeum opened in Rhode Island, the oldest lending library in the USA, which still operates in the original building

1759	The British Museum Library, a precursor to the British Library, opened in London
1791	The card catalogue system (*see page 97*) was developed during the French Revolution
1793	The Royal Danish Library in Copenhagen was opened to the public
1800	President John Adams signed legislation creating the Library of Congress
1814	The British invaded Washington and burned down the Library of Congress, with the loss of some 5,000 books
1833	The first public library in North America opened in Peterborough, New Hampshire
1841	The London Library, the largest independent lending library in the world, opened
1850	The Public Libraries Act was passed in Britain giving local authorities the right to establish free public libraries
1853	The first Librarian's Convention was held in New York City; eighty delegates attended
1857	One of the first mobile libraries began circulating (*see page 53*) in Cumbria
1870	The US Copyright Act, requiring that two copies of all US publications be sent to the Library of Congress, was passed

1876	Melvil Dewey published guidelines for his Dewey Decimal system of classification (*see page 28*)
1879	Electric lighting was installed in the reading room of the British Museum
1883	Andrew Carnegie (*see page 32*) established his first public library in his hometown of Dunfermline, Scotland
1887	Melvil Dewey created the School of Library Economy to train future librarians
1897	The new larger Library of Congress, the Thomas Jefferson building in Washington DC, opened to the public
1911	New York Public Library opened to the public
1926	At the American Library Association Conference, the use of microfilm for recording and storing documents was sanctioned
1939–41	President Franklin D. Roosevelt established the Presidential Library system (*see page 52*)
1960	Machine readable cataloguing (MARC) developed, which allows books to be digitally catalogued
1971	Project Gutenberg established as the first free online library of e-books

1973	The British Library was established by an Act of Parliament
1979	PLR was established in Britain, ensuring writers are paid every time a book is taken out of the library (*see page 16*)
1995	JSTOR founded, a digital library for academic journals
1997	The British Library Reading Rooms in St Pancras opened
2002	The Google Books Project was established to digitize books and make them available online for free

INDEX

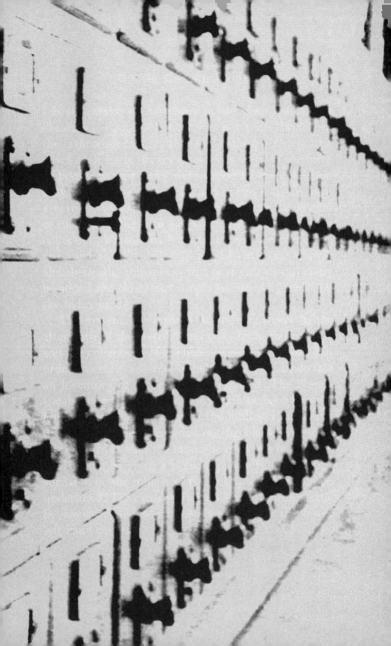